CONVERSATIONS
WITH THE
WORLD

JOHN TUSA

ABOUT THE AUTHOR

John Tusa, aged 54, was born in Zlin, Czechoslovakia, where his father was an executive with Bata, the international shoe company. The family moved to England in 1939 when his father was appointed Managing Director of the company's British subsidiary. They did not return to Czechoslovakia and John Tusa became a British citizen in 1947.

John Tusa joined the BBC in 1960, having taken a first class degree in modern history at Trinity College, Cambridge. After two years in radio, television and the regions, he became a current affairs producer with BBC External Services and in 1967 started work as a freelance broadcaster. Later he presented both *The World Tonight* on Radio 4 and *24 Hours* on the (English-language) World Service, and in 1979 he began his long association with the *Newsnight* programme on BBC2. In 1983 John Tusa was the Royal Television Society's TV Journalist of the Year and a year later he won BAFTA's Richard Dimbleby Award. He took up his post as Managing Director, BBC External Broadcasting (now World Service) in September 1986.

John Tusa is married with two sons. Besides work for the BBC he has written two books with his wife, Ann – *The Nuremberg Trial* (1983) and *The Berlin Blockade* (1988).

CONVERSATIONS WITH THE WORLD

BBC BOOKS

To my predecessors, whose determination and devotion
to the principles and practice of broadcasting independence
created the conditions in which World Service operates today.

Published by BBC Books,
a division of BBC Enterprises Limited,
Woodlands, 80 Wood Lane, London W12 0TT
First published 1990

© John Tusa 1990

ISBN 0 563 36006 2

Set in Trump Medieval by Ace Filmsetting Ltd, Frome
Printed and bound in Great Britain by Redwood Press Ltd, Melksham
Cover printed by Richard Clay Ltd, Norwich

CONTENTS

INTRODUCTION

In the three months before I took over as Managing Director of the External Services (as they were then called), I had the rare privilege of visiting and talking to all the 37 language services that currently constitute Britain's voice abroad. During that process I was especially struck by the Polish Service. The office of the programme organiser had photographs of all his predecessors hung on the walls. No other service did this and I was impressed by the proper sense of continuity and history that this simple act displayed.

The World Service as a whole was, and is, a repository of anecdotage about itself, and its very editorial and managerial freedom is the product of important historical incidents. Many were, I felt, in danger of being forgotten, and in the course of my first three years in the job I found myself turning to these case studies as subjects for lectures or essays. They usually made good copy; they crystallised my own thoughts about how I should defend the positions that my predecessors had established; and, as a historian by training, I found the process of tracing the historical evolution of World Service comforting and reassuring. The principles – of editorial freedom and managerial responsibility – were sound in themselves, and the occasions on which they had been established or defended left me with an even greater admiration for those who had taken a stand and maintained them.

The resulting essays, which make up the body of this book, survey the major *loci classici* of World Service experience. I hope that they will keep alive in a brief form the collective historical memory on which an organisation such as the World Service depends. Anyone who wants to go more deeply into the events should read Gerard Mansell's authoritative and wide-ranging history of World Service, *Let Truth be Told.* I was lucky enough to learn my journalism from Gerry Mansell as a General Trainee at Bush

House in the early 1960s. His book is an invaluable source of reference, and his teaching continues through these pages.

The last three pieces are of a different kind. They are the direct result of the word-processing revolution in the shape of the Tandy lap-top portable computer. I forget now who first suggested that I should take one of these with me on my travels. Whoever it was, I should like to thank them now. I soon discovered that the Tandy is the near-perfect companion, always available to fill in those dull half hours in a 'plane when reading is too much effort, those airport delays, or as a substitute for a human companion. It is somebody to tell about the day, which can be preserved, what's more, in a form I can read myself. There is an additional factor. I have tried to avoid routine travels, to conferences without point, to places without edge to them. Although not actively involved in journalism any more – for the time being – I have been extremely lucky in the situations I have encountered. The historic weekend of the Polish election in June 1989; the intense debate in Pakistan about how to handle Afghanistan after the Soviet withdrawal; the experience of desolation and attempted reconstruction of post-Amin Uganda. When I showed my raw journals from these trips to my editor, Heather Holden-Brown, I urged her not to be polite. It was her judgement that they had an interest which justified their inclusion in this collection. The responsibility for them is of course wholly my own.

I am grateful to Heather for being a critical eye for these essays, and full of admiration for Kelly Davis who did as much adaptation of them from the spoken style to the written as she could with skill and sensitivity. Michael Williams, who is himself a walking repository of Bush House memories, has often produced the crucial texts and telling quotes to give point to an argument or colour to a story. If we were in Japan he would qualify as a National Treasure. Mary Welch, the Bush House Librarian, has located documents and books, often working to a very approximate definition of what I thought I was looking for. My secretaries, Lisette Jones and Elizabeth Rose, have turned what I can only call messy typescripts into models of clarity with a speed that it was easy to take for granted. Diana Burnett, my Personal Assistant, ordered my diary, protected my time and guarded my energies in a way that allowed me the time to do the writing. If ever anybody is a personal organiser, it is she. I am most grateful to all of them.

Finally, I want to thank those who travelled with me on the three journeys covered here. Andrew Taussig, Controller, European Services, comes like me from Central Europe. He was the ideal companion with whom to share the spectacle in Poland of a Communist regime collapsing under its own contradictions. In Uganda, Eileen Mullen, Senior International Publicity Officer, World Service, stoically endured the possibility that she might find herself explaining to the press that the Managing Director had vanished in the bush. She dealt with the crisis with exemplary professionalism. Finally, it was a rare and special privilege to travel through Pakistan with my wife, Ann. The satisfaction of unpeeling the often brutal complexities of Pakistan–Afghan diplomacy and politics with the perception of her historian's eyes gave the journey a rare intensity. We usually don't have the opportunity to travel together in this way. I am lucky that on this occasion we did.

Re-reading these essays is a powerful reminder of the speed with which change has torn through Eastern Europe and the Soviet Union. Many assumptions appear very different even two years after they were first made. I have not re-written them because that would have created a misleading impression of far-sightedness on my part. Besides, the atmosphere of the time served as the appropriate frame for the principles under discussion; those principles, I believe, still hold good.

I should add a word about the title 'BBC World Service'. Until 1988, the institution was called the 'BBC External Services'. Within that body, the 24-hour-a-day English language network was called the 'BBC World Service'. Since most people referred to the entire institution as 'BBC World Service', we decided to yield gracefully and adopted that title for the whole activity in 1988. The English language network is now therefore 'World Service in English'. I have left the reference to 'External Services' in the text as it would be anachronistic to remove them.

John Tusa

I

INTERNATIONAL RADIO THE BROAD VIEW

THE USES AND ABUSES OF INTERNATIONAL BROADCASTING

I f you buy a short-wave radio you can pass many a happy hour searching the wave bands and stumbling on a bewildering variety of broadcasts and broadcasters. This is the community of the international broadcasters: Radio Moscow, Voice of America, Radio Beijing, Deutsche Welle, Radio France International, Radio Netherlands and so on, including of course the BBC External Services.

In 1986, the Americans – that includes Voice of America, Radio Free Europe and Radio Liberty – put out some 2355 hours of airtime each week though that has certainly been reduced since because of budget cuts. The Soviet Union broadcast 2272 hours; Radio Beijing 1554; Deutsche Welle and Deutschlandfunk some 821; and the BBC came fifth as we had done since 1970 with some 733 hours, though it was around 750 in 1987. There are another 22 international broadcasters who transmitted between 200 and 500 hours per week in 1987. Taken together, that is an awful lot of airtime.

To put it bluntly, we do not have enough airtime, or frequencies, to go round. A conference in Geneva tried to devise a system of rationing and equal access to the airwaves in March 1987. It failed because it could not produce a system which worked, which would be observed and which bore much relation to the traditional interests of both the major broadcasters and the minor ones (such as Brazil) who use short wave for domestic transmissions.

So each week some 15 000 hours of international broadcasting create a cacophony on the airwaves and often cancel one another out. To be accurate, many of those hours of broadcasting are heard only in the studio; their transmitters are so weak, their targeting so poor, and their editorial content so indifferent that their audience can hardly be counted.

Nevertheless we all continue to do it, to spend millions of pounds on it – in our case £115.5 million in 1988. Why? And why are there as many ways of broadcasting as there are stations? It is the range and variety of this output that I want to discuss in this essay. I will start with a look at the main strands of international broadcasting as defined in the early days and during the Second World War; then I will try to describe the main types of broadcasting currently in operation; finally I will sketch out some different programme mixes that are used in these varied broadcasting schools.

But to begin at the beginning: there have always been two starkly contrasted views of the uses to which international broadcasting should be put. Is nation speaking peace unto nation or is it very often a pack of lies? These are the strands which still colour all international broadcasting today – strands which I shall call the 'idealistic' and the 'ideological' – and which are the theme of this essay. The idealistic strand was expressed at the opening of the first transmission of the BBC Empire Service on 19 December 1932. J. H. Whitley, the Chairman of the Governors, said:

> *This wireless, one of the great gifts of Providence to mankind, is a trust of which we are humble ministers. Our prayer is that nothing mean or cheap may lessen its value and that its message may bring happiness and comfort to those who listen.*

Reith called it

> *an instrument of almost incalculable importance in the social and political life of the community. Its influence will more and more be felt in the daily life of the individual, in almost every sphere of activity, in affairs national and international.*

And he added: 'The service as a whole is dedicated to the best interests of mankind.' Such statements strike an answering chord of sympathy and recognition in the minds of all of us today. These are still the operating principles for a liberal theory of international broadcasting.

There were, and are, other definitions and they came into being at almost exactly the same time as Reith's and Whitley's. For, as a former director of the Voice of America observed:

*Communication systems are neutral. They have neither
conscience nor morality: only a history. They will broadcast
truth or falsehood with equal facility. Man communicating
with man poses not a problem of how to say it, but, more
fundamentally, what is he to say?*

Others in those early days had a very clear idea of 'what to say' on
this new medium.

Two years before the BBC Empire Service took to the air in 1932
– it had taken five years of negotiation and failure to persuade the
government to underwrite this venture, before the BBC reluctantly decided to find the money itself – the new Soviet Union
was well ahead of Britain in understanding the importance of
international radio and following up this understanding with
action. Radio Centre Moscow was already broadcasting in 50 languages and dialects. Its governing principle was not Reith's service in the 'interests of mankind' but the idea that 'a great and holy
hatred of capitalism is necessary' – a clear expression of the ideological principle of broadcasting.

On 1 April 1935 Nazi Germany turned its attention to dissemi-
nating worldwide the ideas of the Third Reich. Hitler had already
identified psychological dislocation as an essential part of total
war. 'Our strategy', he said, 'is to destroy the enemy from within,
to conquer him through himself. Mental confusion, contradictions of feeling, indecision, panic – these are our weapons.' How
better to sow such feelings of psychological demoralisation than
through the new method of radio? As a former head of the governing German Radio Chamber put it, in ecstatic terms:

*We spell radio with three exclamation marks because we are
possessed in it of a miraculous power – the strongest weapon
ever given to the spirit – that opens hearts and does not stop at
the borders of cities and does not turn back before closed doors;
that jumps rivers, mountains and seas; that is able to force
peoples under the spell of one powerful spirit.*

And he concluded: 'Radio is the most ideal instrument of propaganda.'

The contrasts could not be more striking: Reith and Whitley
laying the new gift of communication, in a suitably awe-struck

way, at the feet of the audience; Moscow directing its broadcasts to serve one political purpose – the class war; and Berlin projecting the single will of the leader throughout the world to serve its own ends. It was the idealists – Reith and Whitley – versus the ideologues – Lenin and Hitler; the former speaking peace, the latter speaking propaganda. The struggle continues to this day.

Sadly, throughout the 1930s, it was the ideologues rather than the idealists who were first to take advantage of the new medium. In the case of the Nazi Reichsender broadcasts, they targeted Germans living abroad with thoroughness and some significant success. Aware of the large number of Germans throughout the Americas, Reichsender approached them in several ways: the short-wave transmissions to Latin America warned of the dangers of dollar diplomacy and the obscenity of the American rich; a regular radio news service was supplied free to local newspapers; and by 1937, Argentina alone was carrying some 500 rebroadcast German radio programmes per year at a time when those from Britain could be counted on the fingers of one hand.

From time to time Reichsender got its tone wrong, as when it addressed its American German listeners with the coy – or threatening – question: 'Hans, do you know that the German Reichstag has its eyes on you?', to be followed quickly with the more reassuring: 'And now Hans, listen to a song from your home.' Or the all-too-friendly address to Tasmania: 'Hello, Tasmania, beautiful apple isle.'

However, there was nothing comic in the radio propaganda barrage directed against the Austrians before the union of Austria and Germany (the Anschluss) or the Czechs when they were compelled to surrender the Sudetenland to Germany. Immediately after the Anschluss, Dr Goebbels arranged for 25 000 radio sets to be distributed among the poor so that they could keep in touch with the world view of their new masters. And after the fall of France, the Germans imposed armistice terms which included the silencing of France's wireless transmitters.

The ideologues devoted a good deal of radio effort to attacking one another. Radio Centre Moscow specialised in details of the extra-marital activities of Nazi leaders such as Goebbels, a habit that led first to an attempt at jamming by the Third Reich; then to a ban on listening; and finally to Russians, Poles or Slovaks living within the Reich's frontiers being forbidden to own radios. 'Hier Spricht Moskau' attempted to turn the propaganda war back on the Communists with its detailed descriptions of the poverty of Soviet life. But both sides were capable of demonstrating an admirable flexibility in 1939. At 4 pm on the day when the Molotov–Ribbentrop Pact was signed, Radio Stuttgart was scheduled to emit a particularly vitriolic attack on the Soviet Union entitled 'I accuse Moscow'. It never found the ether, being rapidly replaced by a 15-minute concert of Russian folk music.

Britain, at this stage, was far behind. It took a challenge by the least of the ideologues, Fascist Italy, to a major area of British interest, the Middle East, to stir the British government into action.

Mussolini's aim was simple enough – to undermine Britain in the Arab World. He faced two major obstacles. Arabs had practically no radios and very few clocks. How could they listen? And if they could hear, how would they know when to tune in? Italian ingenuity and effort should not be underrated. The first problem was solved by distributing sets tuned to one station alone – Radio Bari in Southern Italy. The second was simpler. Used as Arabs are to saying their prayers according to the position of the sun, so Radio Bari's transmissions were announced in terms of sunrise and sunset. Mussolini's strategy was brilliantly successful.

It took several representations by British diplomats abroad, to the effect that anti-British sentiment was seriously inflamed by these broadcasts, before the government decided to fund the BBC Arabic Service on 3 January 1938. This was the first of the vernacular services to start from Britain, and its fiftieth anniversary was celebrated in January 1988. Once Britain entered short-wave broadcasting, our expansion was rapid. But why were politicians so slow in appreciating the significance of this new opportunity?

Writing in 1957, in a book called *Propaganda*, Professor Lindley Fraser, the former head of the BBC German Service and one of the most influential leaders of the BBC's wartime broadcasts, answered the question like this:

Advocates of external propaganda in Great Britain always had (and still have) to face the vociferous hostility of certain

*sections of the press and of public opinion and the influence of
this hostility upon governmental decisions has not necessarily
been less important because its grounds have never been
formulated. For most of the inter-war period, the only form of
external publicity tolerated by the British authorities was the
British Council, a strictly cultural body which most unjustly
tended to be the target of attack from two opposite sides: from
anti-propaganda newspapers which professed to regard its work
as a pure waste of taxpayers' money, and from suspicious
groups abroad which suspected its branches and institutes of
being centres of espionage.*

I am sure that Professor Fraser's analysis is correct, although I
do not think one can use the term propaganda in the value-free
way that he did 30 years ago. After all, you could write the very
same thing today. But what concerns me and others is that there is
as little sense of urgency now as there was in the 1930s, or in 1957
when Fraser wrote. In fact communicating with the world outside
should be a matter of higher rather than lower priority. Britain
cannot permit its competitors to seize the commanding heights in
this field without regretting the consequences later (especially as
we are very good at this activity when we are given funds to do it).
A strategy of investing in success, in not selling Britain short,
should lead to a greater investment in cultural diplomacy rather
than a policy which says – for no apparent reason – that what we
spend now is 'about right'. For all we know – in the absence of
arguments or analysis to the contrary – what we spend now may
well be 'about wrong'.

In the end, the output of the wartime ideological powers was
destroyed by reality. Though attempting to manipulate the truth,
they were defeated by the facts. For Hitler, the Fourth Front of the
war was controlled by the maxim 'Words are acts'. He was of
course proved utterly wrong. If words could have staved off
defeat, the Führer would still be on the podium of history. As it is,
the acts of the war made the words of wartime propagandists
empty, discreditable and discredited.

Was there a better way? Were the idealistic broadcasters more
successful in sticking to their principles and to the truth even at
times when the truth was a record of bleak and continuous

setback? The evidence is that there *was* a better way and that its practitioners trod it with greater effectiveness and far more personal dignity, though not without their own difficulties and doubts.

In 1957 Professor Fraser listed the essential ingredients of a successful propaganda effort, though as I have said, the word propaganda is not one we can use today in a neutral sense. These ingredients can be summed up in the words 'truth' and 'consistency' – principles which require great skill to turn into effective broadcasting. The demands of truth during the war led to an honest admission of British defeats. They could hardly be concealed. But they were presented within an argument – says Fraser – which went as follows:

> *Yes, we have taken a beating so far. But we are not defeated. Hitler has predicted that he will win and will win soon. His victories so far have cost him heavily and guarantee that the war, far from being short, will be long. Hitler will lose a protracted war and the longer it is protracted, the worse the defeat in the end.*

'This line of argument', concedes Fraser, ' must have seemed far-fetched indeed to European audiences during the months preceding the evacuation from Dunkirk.' Yet, we see now, it was intrinsically capable of being true. It was, after all, not provable in advance, and the longer the war dragged on, the more credible, indeed accurate, it was seen to be. So the first criterion – truthfulness – was met.

The second was consistency. This is less obvious, because it involves not so much consistency for one audience as consistency for all audiences. The message cannot be differently shaped for different countries and populations, for people eavesdrop where they can and if they discover that the message is specially tailored with a particular audience in mind, then both the message and the messenger will be discredited.

Various parts of the British output to Germany could afford to be more robust in their approach while still sticking to the canons of truthfulness. 'Oh that mine enemy would write a book,' sighed Job. In the war, mine enemy had not only written a book, he and his colleagues made endless speeches. The BBC had recordings of the main ones. As the war continued it was possible to measure the warnings and claims of the Nazi leaders against the actual events as they unfolded. Small teams of producers sat listening to Hitler's latest claims and then rushed to his previous speeches to identify the earlier remark which contradicted the later one out of his own mouth. It was propaganda; it was true; and it must have been enormous fun.

It was also very frustrating. Effective as the German Service was – and Fraser does not claim anything more than a very marginal impact on the conduct of the war, still less its outcome – it seems that programmes such as the Eastern Service, in which George Orwell worked, were far less effective; indeed, at the outset, they were very slow off the mark. On 6 October 1939, the *Daily Telegraph* wrote from Delhi: 'German propaganda in English excellently received. Listeners wait vainly for refutation from London or Delhi.'

What they got instead, according to Kingsley Martin in the *New Statesman*, was:

> comments on the death of such celebrities as Ethel M. Dell and on the valuable contribution to British defence afforded by a group of Australian footballers who filled some sandbags before sailing for their homes. Before the war and even after it, British broadcasting to India consisted almost exclusively of British music hall music, cafe orchestra music and sentimental talk in spite of the fact that Indians dislike European music and think music hall entertainments vulgar.

Not much competition for the broadcasts from Berlin of Subhas Chandra Bose, the militant Indian nationalist, calling for Indians to rise up and overthrow the Raj.

Orwell became an Empire Talks Assistant in the Indian Section shortly after Kingsley Martin wrote the above article, but much of his work did not appear to be a significant advance on Ethel M. Dell. The names he brought to the microphone were certainly top drawer: Joseph Needham on Science, Capitalism and Fascism; Arthur Calder-Marshall on Contemporary English Literature; talks by T. S. Eliot, E. M. Forster and Stephen Spender. They were distinguished but were they relevant to the matter in hand? Would they convince sceptical Indians that Britain's fight against

Fascism was their fight too, rather than their opportunity to seize independence?

Fortunately, another aspect of Orwell's activity was far more relevant to this task – that is to say the weekly talks on events in the news that he gave from December 1941 to March 1943. It was here that the idealistic broadcaster revealed his character most fully over the ideologue. George Orwell was not as funny as Tokyo Rose (see the next essay), less apparently prescient than Lord Haw-Haw, but was he more effective? Very early, on 17 January 1942, Orwell addressed the question of propaganda itself. Both the Fascist enemies, Germany and Japan, he noted were very adept at it:

> *They cover up every military move by spreading misleading rumours beforehand, they use threats and bribes with equal skill and they are entirely cynical in promising everything to everybody. To the rich they promise bigger profits and to the poor they promise higher wages. To the coloured races they promise liberty, and simultaneously they appeal to the white races to combine for the exploitation of the coloured races.*

And then Orwell offered a foolproof test to probe the nature of the propaganda being broadcast – compare what the propagandists do with what they say. As he put it:

> *The one safe rule is to remember that acts count for more than words and that the Japanese must be judged not by what they promise to do tomorrow in India or Burma but what they did yesterday and are still doing in Korea, Manchuria and China.*

And for the next two years Orwell patiently drew his audience's attention to that great and growing gap between Fascist claims and Fascist acts. I do not know how much contact there was between the German and the Indian Services at the BBC but it is reassuring to see Professor Fraser's axioms being so consistently put into practice.

So, what, in the end, is at stake in the debate about international communications? In December 1941, America's newsmen gathered to honour the reporting of the London blitz by the greatest of war correspondents, Ed Murrow. In his eulogy, Archibald MacLeish, the poet and Librarian of Congress, touched on the importance of equality between the broadcaster and the listener:

> *There were some in this country, Murrow, who did not want the people of America to hear the things you had to say . . . who did not wish to remember that . . . freedom of speech . . . is freedom also to hear . . . to assure people a chance to hear the truth, the unpleasant truth as well as the reassuring truth, the dangerous truth as well as the comforting truth . . .*

That was well said then, and well to remember now. Who could be more antithetical than Hitler and Orwell?

There is one other revealing antithesis that has emerged. Writing in *Mein Kampf*, Adolf Hitler had asserted, 'In wartime, words are acts.' Writing for the BBC Indian Section, George Orwell wrote, 'The one safe rule to remember is that acts count for more than words.' Orwell was right. The idealists won. Words cannot create facts; they can only describe them. That is the only sound basis on which nation can truly speak peace unto nation.

Today, as international broadcasting has proliferated, so have the forms which it takes and the theories advanced to justify those forms. These various forms have been shaped by the experience of short-wave broadcasting which itself has completely contradictory characteristics for operator and listener.

Short-wave broadcasting is very expensive for the operator; while short-wave listening is very cheap for the listener. Short-wave broadcasting is the most public form of communication for the operator, notoriously difficult to control and often reaching parts of the world no other medium can reach; it is also the most private form of listening for the audience, allowing access to a world the politicians would wish to deny them. Short-wave broadcasting is often a public and national expression of state power; yet short-wave listening affords the listener the most potent way of challenging and circumventing that state power. Finally, short-wave broadcasting exists because governments ascribe to it a value in promoting their overall state policies. Meanwhile the short-wave listener tunes in for reasons of his or her own, notoriously impervious to the direct or indirect message which is the prime motive of the original broadcast.

Short-wave broadcasting is, in essence, anarchic – it leaps boundaries, defies regulations, scatters forbidden thoughts and challenges otherwise unchallengeable authorities. It is essentially humanistic, allowing the individual to make his or her own decisions about their view of the world; it opens minds; defies collective regimentation and, out of the darkling confusion of the ether, offers a dialogue of ideas between broadcaster and listener.

From an élite form of communication reaching miniscule audiences, for relatively trivial purposes, short-wave broadcasting has grown into a truly mass form of communication which enables millions of people around the world to choose what they wish to hear. It is profoundly democratic. With regulation, restriction and censorship all around us, short wave is surely the last great free medium.

That is what short wave *can* do. What *does* it do in practice?

At its simplest, a nation wants to speak to its nationals abroad. Around the world are scattered groups of expatriate nationals, some exiled out of necessity, some who have emigrated by choice, yet many who still cling to their national identity. They want to hear that home is still there; that home is still as it was or, preferably, better than they remember it. The mother country feels a residual obligation to the offspring who keep a little corner of a distant land forever Ruritania.

As Sir William Haley, a former Director-General of the BBC, put it in 1950: 'The purpose was to use this latest, swiftest and perhaps most personal means of communication to forge a link between the homeland and the pioneers in voluntary exile overseas.' More colourfully, a British pamphleteer of the 1930s mused lyrically over the link between broadcaster and the distant audience:

> There is something magnificently romantic in the thought that men on trek in the desert or the jungle will be able, by switching a little lever, to listen to the dance bands of sophisticated civilisation. I have known many of these lonely pioneers who are seeking 'something beyond the ranges'. Despite their years of wandering they nearly all have a nostalgia for home.

This need still exists though it is by no means the most important role for a transnational broadcaster. Even so, every international broadcaster, at least to some extent, still serves the purpose of reaching out a reassuring voice to the national abroad or the co-religionary. In this function, the external broadcaster is a kind of umbilical link between 'mother' and 'child' abroad. As the comparison implies, it is sometimes a difficult relationship, with the expatriate – as we call them in Britain – making demands of the broadcaster which he or she cannot fulfil. We cannot always present a picture of a Britain without blemish. We will not pretend that it is a society that has not altered and will not change. At its best, the relationship with the 'expat' is one where the citizen abroad hears, with approval, a broadcast from his own country. At its worst, the relationship becomes fractious, with the expatriate resentful that the country he or she willingly left has decided to do things differently in his or her absence. Radio Japan provides a very positive example, with its powerful sense of wishing to embrace all the Japanese people scattered around in the world. The Japanese have a very strong sense of cultural and national cohesion; it comes naturally to them to use radio as a way of keeping the national family in one sense always united.

The second major role of the transnational broadcaster is the projection of the nation and its activities. (I should add at this point that I am listing these functions in a descriptive way without any implication as to their relative importance. I leave it to others to decide how to vary the proportions of these various functions in their own broadcasting.)

The concept of national projection is simple: 'We broadcast from Ruritania; we must tell the world about Ruritania; by extension, the world should listen.' An extreme form of this approach is exemplified in the world's first substantial effort in transnational television, the American government-funded 'Worldnet'. This is openly a way of projecting America and US government policy to the world abroad, very often defined as journalists and opinion-formers. Thus, Secretaries of State will appear regularly and hold intercontinental news conferences. Even in Worldnet's more orthodox magazine programming, the main drive is to tell the world about America. The aim is no doubt laudable and certainly understandable. But is it likely to succeed? Our experience of broadcasters who are required by statute to talk principally about their country to the world is that they do not get much of an audience, and that has certainly been true of Worldnet.

Yet it is clearly not acceptable or sensible to say nothing about the country from which you are broadcasting. Our own activity in BBC External Services is governed by the interplay between two of the elements in our statement of objectives. The first says that we must be 'credible' and various other things besides. A secondary one says that we should reflect British life, society, industry and so on. Of course we do reflect them. But we do not do so in an isolated way. We treat British writers, artists, actors, industrialists and scientists as we treat those of the world beyond. We talk of artists in programmes which also talk of foreign artists, for you can only see the significance of one in the context of the others.

Equally, you can only talk credibly of British science or industry if you set it in the context of foreign competition. They live, work, compete and exchange ideas in a robust international environment every day; they would not gain from being isolated in a protected broadcasting environment. Our broadcasting about Britain gains in credibility because it does not give special treatment to British activities. They earn their place on the air in competition with the rest of the world. That is why we are credible and so are they. The more narrowly you interpret the instruction to broadcast about your home country, the less appealing you are to your audience.

The third role of transnational broadcasting is propaganda. I use the word here in a technical sense and without value judgement, though you may guess where my instincts lie.

I can say without much fear of contradiction that of the world's 21 leading broadcasters – that's those with more than 300 broadcast hours a week – 21 are committed, by ideology and without apology, to propaganda. It constitutes a total of 7170 hours a week, certainly half as much again as the time devoted to informational broadcasting.

I define propaganda as broadcasting wholly at the service of the state, wholly in the hands of the government and wholly intended to serve the policy aims defined by state and government. It is the broadcasting of persuasion, the broadcasting of a world where black contests with white, the broadcasting of friend versus foe, the broadcasting of a Manichean world where those who are not for us are against us and the purpose of the broadcaster is to change the latter into the former.

It is rash for anybody to write this off as a waste of time or money. After all, if the USSR devotes 2174 hours a week to propaganda, China 1554 hours, North Korea 548, Albania 452 and Iran 354 hours, then there must be something in it. Undoubtedly (and not only among governments which see the control of public information as desirable politically), propaganda, or something close to it, is appreciated in theory even if governments cannot set a value on it in practice.

But propaganda seems to me to be the supreme case of one-way broadcasting – the listener is there to receive what the broadcaster thinks he or she should hear. The exchange between them is limited; how could it be otherwise? The broadcasters cannot change their minds; they have a line to pursue. The listeners can only take it or leave it, and most of the time they leave it. The bitter experience of Radio Beijing is instructive. They have admitted that the hectoring propaganda of the Cultural Revolution years lost them most of their audience. And they have since been searching anxiously for ways to build it up.

I have no doubt that the broadcasting of propaganda will continue in the years ahead. Many governments will not be capable of any other response to the continuing effectiveness and penetration of foreign broadcasters into the awareness of their own audiences and hence into their politics. The irony, which has never been a secret, is that the most effective of such broadcasters do not offer propaganda. They offer – in various ways – information.

The fourth main role of transnational radio I shall call broadly information. As I cannot answer for others, I shall describe how we in the BBC External Services tackle this task.

The information we broadcast concerns the world; its events; its politics; its struggles; everything that makes a difference to how we live, and in all too many cases to how some die, and how many suffer.

Why do we broadcast such information? Because freedom of information (or truth), like peace, is indivisible. If you believe that a just political order and a properly responsive political society can only function with the co-operation and assistance of free information media at home; if, in short, justice cannot be based on a lie, then that principle must apply equally abroad. The words of Lord Bridge, Britain's senior Law Lord, and a former head of the

Security Commission (the body that supervises Britain's security services), are relevant here. Giving his reasons for wanting the injunction banning publication of the Peter Wright book *Spycatcher* to be lifted (a view on which he was out-voted by three other Law Lords), Lord Bridge delivered this observation on the relationship between falsehood and tyranny:

> *Freedom of speech is always the first casualty under a totalitarian regime. Such a regime cannot afford to allow the free circulation of information and ideas among its citizens. Censorship is the indispensable tool to regulate what the public may and what they may not know. The present attempt to insulate the public in this country from information which is freely available elsewhere is a very significant step down that dangerous road.*

How much more do those views apply to harmonious international relations?

Furthermore, correct and peaceful relations between states cannot be based on one side being presented as the owner of the whole truth and the other side as jackals, murderers, lackeys, Great Satans, or whatever the modish phrases of denunciation may be. Conflicts cannot be settled if one side is always right and insists on telling its own people that the other side is the enemy and always wrong. International relations require a flow of information that is free and truthful. Britain defines this as being in the national interest, and that is why we broadcast as we do.

One of our objectives is that our broadcasts should include 'a credible, unbiased, reliable, balanced and independent news service'. I believe we are privileged to have to work to such an admirable definition. It imposes on us a responsibility not simply to the country from which we come but to the audience to which we broadcast.

Most fundamentally, I believe that what distinguishes this informational approach to transnational broadcasting is the relationship with the audience. It sets the broadcaster on an equal footing with the audience. The broadcaster cannot tell the listener whether to listen, when to listen, how to listen, or what to think. The broadcaster depends entirely on the listener deciding to tune in. The relationship is human, humanistic, respectful, tolerant. It is in essence a conversation, both remote and intimate, about the great issues of the world and the great ideas. Because it puts the transmitter and receiver on an equal intellectual footing, it attracts the audience in a way that the hectoring tone of the propagandist can never do. And it is only on the basis of respect for the audience that transnational radio can enable nation to speak peace until nation, and expect to be listened to.

Finally, how do these different philosophies translate themselves into programmes?

Some networks, such as Voice of America (VOA) Europe or Radio Monte Carlo, use the bait of a heavy diet of pop music to catch and keep an audience, arguing that they also take in the news bulletins and occasional information programmes within the stream. VOA Europe, by the way, has a heavier propaganda role than its mother station; it is based on the proposition that what is called the 'successor' generation in Europe has not lived through the formative years of the post-war period, that it is ignorant of the historical experience which has created a divided Europe, ignorant of and somewhat soft towards a smiling Soviet Union, and vulnerable to propaganda against the United States which may appear stronger in military terms. If this generation is not to drift into neutralism, the argument goes, they must be kept alert and informed about what's really going on in the world. My own view is that this is a misconception of the Western European experience and that the broadcasting approach which covers everything in a layer of pop music treacle is not likely to yield the desired results in the long run.

It is also the case with Radio Monte Carlo, which broadcasts in Arabic with a constant stream of pop, that although it has a glib superficial appeal, its news is simply not good enough. Listeners have discovered that it is not as reliable as it should be and they almost always check with a broadcaster they trust such as the BBC Arabic Service.

Then there are the 'Alternative Home Service' stations such as Radio Free Europe and Radio Liberty. Each broadcasts for almost the entire day to the Eastern bloc and the Soviet Union respectively. Their fundamental approach is simple; 'these countries cannot hear anything but what the state allows them to hear. We will make good that deficiency.' Events such as the riot in 1987 of factory-workers at Brasov in Romania were just the kind of incident that these stations thrive on. They are effective. They have large audiences.

What is wrong with such an approach? Mainly that it falls into the hands of émigrés only, and émigrés of one political persuasion; and, more importantly, that they get stuck in the groove of one type of analysis: 'These regimes are oppressive, incompetent, dangerous and untrustworthy; they cannot merely be opposed; they should be abolished.' It imposes a dangerous rigidity of outlook on the broadcasters which sometimes leaves them stranded when events move faster than their analytical outlook permits.

Finally, there are the 'wolves in sheep's clothing' stations. It is amazing how many World Services sprang up after the BBC had created theirs. The Radio Moscow World Service has 'Midnight in Moscow' rather than 'Lilliburlero'; the Kremlin chimes rather than Big Ben; and a style of delivery which, though often Americanised, aspires to the gravitas of the best BBC announcers. Radio South Africa adopts very English voices, with very English accents, and often uses BBC correspondents in its current affairs programmes to add to the confusion. Imitation is the sincerest form of flattery; it is good to know that our competitors use us as a yardstick of style with which to try and build their own credibility.

Which of all these views and styles constitute the uses and which the abuses of international broadcasting? I believe that we do use it properly. But then I would, wouldn't I?

This chapter was first delivered as 'The Uses and Abuses of International Broadcasting' at the London School of Economics Seminar on 2 December 1987.

'WHEN LOUD RUMOUR SPEAKS' – RADIO PROPAGANDA

In the previous essay we discussed the tension between idealism and ideology in transnational broadcasting, and the complex question of propaganda. Now I wish to return to the idealists and the ideologues as they emerged in practice as broadcasters during the war. I intend to look briefly at the very different careers, styles and ends of two famous or infamous Second World War broadcasters: William Joyce, otherwise known as Lord Haw-Haw; and Tokyo Rose, sometimes known as Orphan Annie.

It is of course well known that William Joyce, Lord Haw-Haw, was the master radio propagandist of the Second World War; that he was minutely informed about the most telling details of life in Britain to an often prescient degree; and that he seriously threatened Britain's basic psychological stability during the darkest hours of the war. Yet, on closer examination, all those propositions have to be qualified substantially.

First, was he indeed a master radio propagandist? If that is what he became, it is certainly not how he started. At his audition for a job as a newsreader in the Reichsrundfunk English team in September 1939, Joyce found that the transition from addressing a large public audience in a big hall to addressing an unseen.private audience from a small cubicle was altogether too much. His throat dried up; he over-enunciated; he read too slowly; he took longer than he should to read the test script. He expected to be rejected and he was. As Joyce's future was about to take a dramatically different turn, a radio engineer chipped in to insist that there was *something* in the voice; it could be produced into something better and it was worth another try. The producers decided to test Joyce out on a live bulletin later that day. He was far better than in the actual audition, certainly worth persevering with. He stayed; he spoke; he became a legend.

Second, was he Lord Haw-Haw? Well, not to start with. It was on 14 September 1939 that Jonah Barrington of the *Daily Express* wrote of the German broadcasts to Britain from Zeesen: 'A gent I'd like to meet is moaning periodically from Zeesen. He speaks English of the haw-haw, dammit-get-out-of-my-way variety and his strong suit is gentlemanly indignation.' Four days later Barrington cashed in on his clever phrase and upgraded the thought to a fully fledged character, Lord Haw-Haw, whom he saw in his mind's eye like this: 'From his accent and personality I imagine him with a receding chin, a questing nose, thin, yellow brushed back hair, a monocle, a vacant eye, a gardenia in his button-hole, rather like P. G. Wodehouse's Bertie Wooster.'

Leave aside the fact that William Joyce was shortish, stocky, with a square face, black hair, a massive scar down his cheek, and was never, never mistaken for a gentleman; leave aside the fact that the Bertie Wooster type was precisely the sort of Englishman whom Joyce most derided as representative of the society he wanted to see destroyed; leave aside the fact that the voice which first attracted Jonah Barrington's interest and irritation was that of Norman Baillie-Stewart, a former Seaforth Highlander officer jailed in the war for giving away secrets in 1933. And leave aside the most important fact of all: that Joyce only got his first contract as a newsreader on the very day that Lord Haw-Haw sprang to life in Barrington's column in the *Daily Express.*

Yet if Lord Haw-Haw could not have been Joyce's title at the outset, it was finally appropriated and won by him in the course of time as the most effective and the cleverest of the team of German broadcasters in English. And the broadcasts certainly got under people's skin as curiosity grew about the identity of the broadcasters. BBC monitors noted on September 1939 that there was a new announcer on these stations 'but with a much less ironical tone' than his colleague. On 4 October, Baillie-Stewart was identified by the *Daily Telegraph* after consulting former army colleagues. By May 1940 German Radio was introducing the talks as by Lord Haw-Haw, while still not revealing his true name. On 2 August, British monitors were sufficiently satisfied with the identification to ascribe the title of Lord Haw-Haw to Joyce. Finally, only on 3 April 1941 did Joyce announce himself by name and give his reason for doing what he did: 'I thought that victory, which would preserve existing conditions, would be more damaging to Britain than defeat.'

Now Joyce – Haw-Haw – puzzled and fascinated some of the most notable names in Britain. Harold Hobson wrote in *The Times* that 'that ineffable voice of his, by Cholmondeley-Plantagenet out of Christ Church, has an irresistible fascination'. Rose Macaulay spotted the voice as being provincial and not public school. Lady Cynthia Colville, more acutely still, caught a trans-Atlantic intonation.

For people listened. Late in 1940 the Ministry of Information asked the BBC to assess the audience for broadcasts from Germany. The survey calculated the BBC audience as 23 million listening regularly each day with a further ten million occasional listeners. Reichsrundfunk, by contrast, had six million regular listeners in Britain – probably daily – 18 million occasional listeners and only 11 million who never listened.

The response from this British audience was two-fold. One was ridicule. The Western Brothers turned it into a music hall joke. A letter to the *Daily Mirror* said confidently: 'Haw-Haw gives even an old woman like me a good laugh, as I take all his talks the other way round.' At the other end of the scale, David Lloyd George cautioned: 'The government ought to take notice of every word this man says.' *The Times*, suitably, caught the balance well: 'Much of Lord Haw-Haw's nightly talks is the cause of ribald mirth in countless homes but occasionally one detects a subtler shaft whose effect might well have unfortunate results unless immediately answered.'

The BBC commentary on the 1940 audience survey pinpointed precisely the reason for the appeal of Lord Haw-Haw's broadcasts, for appeal they had:

> *The entertainment value of the broadcasts, their concentration on undeniable evils in this country, their news sense, their presentation, and the publicity they have received in this country, together with the momentum of the habit of listening to them, have all contributed to their establishment as a familiar feature of the social landscape.*

It was a small step from familiarity and habit to credence, no matter how that belief might be veiled in ridicule. Soon Haw-Haw was being credited with intimate knowledge of the most detailed events in Britain, often of a secret nature. There was the matter of the clocks. How did Joyce know that the clock at Banstead was a quarter of an hour slow? Or the clocks in every single village in Sussex? Not to mention the one in East Ham and the Guildhall clock in Cambridge? How did Haw-Haw know that the paint shed in a Midlands factory was being completed and how could he warn his listeners that they should spare themselves the effort as it would shortly be bombed? How could he know about troop movements and convoys and all the damaging things the public heard him say? The only explanation had to be – if these reports were true – that Joyce was fed by an extraordinarily powerful, widespread and diligent Fifth Column in Britain, whose existence and ability to elude the authorities undermined still further the residual sense of security the public enjoyed.

But while it is undoubtedly true that Joyce did damage morale, perhaps to an extent that few cared to admit, it is also a fact – according to those who have examined the scripts – that he did not broadcast many of the statements ascribed to him. He is – according to his biographer J. A. Cole – 'a man who is remembered for what he did not say'. Why did Britons believe what they did? Shakespeare surely has the answer in *Henry IV, Part II*:

> *Open your ears; for which of you will stop*
> *The vent of hearing when loud Rumour speaks?*
> *I, from the orient to the drooping west,*
> *Making the wind my post horse, still unfold*
> *The acts commenced on this ball of earth:*
> *Upon my tongue continual slanders ride,*
> *The which in every language I pronounce,*
> *Stuffing the ears of men with false reports.*
> *I speak of peace, while covert enmity*
> *Under the smile of safety wounds the world:*
> *And who but Rumour, who but only I,*
> *Make fearful musters and prepar'd defence . . .*

Rumour, in other words, fed on what people thought they heard. In this matter, Joyce was one of the first, possibly the most celebrated, but certainly not the last, broadcaster to discover that what you say is one thing; what your listeners think they hear is often quite another.

What *did* Joyce broadcast? In one sense it was standard stuff, emphasising the shortcomings of the government he was attacking. There was anti-semitism, of course, in his character of Sir Izzy Ungeheimer, a tax-evasion expert; Bumbleby Mannering, a hypocritical clergyman adept at shrewd investments in munitions; Sir Jasper Murgatroyd, a dastardly Foreign Office mogul constantly planning Britain's next aggression; and Mr Smith, the tax exile in neutral Switzerland, lambasting the 'rotten workers' and the 'blasted socialists' even as they fought his war for him.

These were all stereotypes of course – crude ones naturally – but the point of stereotypes is that some of the audience are vulnerable to all of them most of the time. They were appropriate enough to stir the unadmitted anxieties of a nation fighting for its life against an enemy who had succeeded in projecting himself as more than merely human. As J. A. Cole puts it: 'They created the image of a diabolical enemy possessing supernormal powers'. At its time, in other words, the propaganda worked, and no amount of fond and humorous recollection of the man they called 'the Humbug of Hamburg, the comic Eau de Cologne', can erase the fact that what is still remembered is what Joyce never said. He was hanged, though, for what he did say.

It is time now to look at a figure who occupied a comparable, if still more confused, place in the ears of the audience around the Pacific. She was Tokyo Rose, star of the aptly named 'Zero Hour', who beguiled her way into the ears of thousands of US GIs with her records, her messages and her artless introduction:

> *Hello boys, this is your favourite enemy again – your little playmate. I understand the butchers of 41st Division are bound for Wewak tonight. Just thought you darling suckers would like to know – the soldiers of Japan are waiting for you there with fixed bayonets.*

Well, so they may have been. The trouble was that 41st Division was bypassing Wewak for a landing on Hollandia. Such inaccuracy was part of Tokyo Rose's charm.

For the rest it was fairly predictable stuff: apparent sympathy for the GIs about the life, the food, the girl-friends, the homes they left behind – and of course the men paying attention to the wives and sweethearts back in the USA. Its intention seemed to be to smother the GIs with kindness, to lower morale through a cloying diet of sentimentality.

Among the broadcasters of Tokyo was Iva Toguri, an American-born Japanese who found herself stranded in Japan when the war broke out, and had adopted the radio name of 'Orphan Annie'. Rather like the Germans and the title Lord Haw-Haw, the name Tokyo Rose was created by the audience, and Tokyo itself only became aware of it as late as March 1944. While some reports attached that title to Iva Toguri, others pointed out that Tokyo Rose's voice was soft and appealing (Toguri's was described by the American who produced her as a 'gin-fog voice, rough almost masculine, anything but a feminine seductive voice'). There was even rivalry for the title between Toguri and her broadcasting colleagues.

It seems that Tokyo Rose existed – like the details of some of Joyce's actual broadcasts – principally in the minds and ears of her listeners. She was an amalgam of a type of broadcasting, rather than one particular broadcaster. That amalgam, at once reassuring and undermining, friendly and hostile, sometimes well-informed, at others badly misled – the oxymoron extended to screaming point – surely fulfils one of the criteria of successful propaganda. It is irrational and contradictory; it triggers subliminal emotions; it deliberately mixes alien elements – 'your favourite enemy', 'you darling suckers' – and creates not so much ridicule at itself, as deep unease in the listener.

Nothing so powerful could be dismissed as being the creation of a collective. It could not be de-personalised. By the end of the war, Tokyo Rose had to exist as a single individual and as American reporters raced to Tokyo after the surrender, the race was on to find her. If she could not be found, she had to be created. And there is some evidence to suggest that that is what happened.

At first all inquiries about the identity of Tokyo Rose drew a blank which was also a wall of ignorance. After all, there were five or six female announcers on 'Zero Hour' – Tokyo Rose could have been any one of them. Finally, a Japanese editor at NHK told two US newsmen from Hearst newspapers that 'perhaps' it was Iva Toguri. They offered her $2000 for an exclusive interview. The first announcement revealing Toguri's role as a broadcaster on 'Zero Hour' contained appropriate reservations: 'Propagandist Tokyo Rose No. 5, one of the Japanese radio sirens who used to amuse Yanks with clumsy propaganda, was revealed yesterday to be Iva Toguri d'Aquino, L.A. born'. That was fair enough, but by the time the Hearst journalists drew up their contract with Toguri for her $2000 exclusive piece, it identified her as 'the one and original "Tokyo Rose" '. Toguri signed the document as 'Iva Ikuko Toguri (Tokyo Rose)'.

The flood of publicity at first appeared exciting, admirable, rewarding. It was rather nice to be 'Tokyo Rose'. It was less pleasant when the questioning by newsmen turned into interrogation by military intelligence, leading to arrest in October 1945. From being a celebrity, Toguri rapidly turned into a traitor. A year later the FBI dropped charges against her on the grounds that Tokyo Rose was 'a composite person with at least a dozen voices'.

Only in 1948, however, after exhaustive analysis of broadcasts and scripts, did the US government charge Toguri and bring her to trial not on the capital charge of treason but on the lesser and somewhat quaint charge of undermining morale, 'creating nostalgia in the minds of the armed forces' and doing so 'intentionally and traitorously'.

Toguri argued that she had broadcast under duress, her radio manner was designed to signal that she did not take the broadcasts seriously and neither should her listeners, and she had stayed loyal to her homeland throughout. A survey of Pacific veterans in the early 1970s found that 84 per cent regarded Tokyo Rose's broadcasts as successful entertainment.

Toguri was sentenced to ten years in jail and a $10 000 fine. She was released after serving six years on 28 January 1956. On 19 January 1977, President Ford's last day in office, they granted Iva Toguri a presidential pardon.

One American newspaper wrote after the sentence that in demonstrating such severity the judge was 'punishing a legend rather than the human being who stood in the dock of justice'. If so, and many would agree with that verdict on the sentence, what was the significance of the legend? In a book about broadcast propaganda written in 1943, *Radio Goes to War*, the American author Charles J. Rolo diagnosed the radio traitors like this. The manner is perhaps somewhat high-flown but written as it was in 1943, I think it captures revealingly the strength of feeling that the enemy radio quisling attracted:

> *The spy, the saboteur, the assassin is a creature of the night, who works silently, alone, underground – and freely risks his life. The radio traitor is ten times more damned. He commits high treason in cold blood daily, almost hourly, for months perhaps years on end. His treachery is public, loud, insistent, and unashamed. His risks, except in the event of defeat or capture – are no greater than those of the ordinary civilian in wartime. And what he seeks to destroy is not one object – a power plant, a factory, a battleship – but his own country; the whole set of institutions, traditions and ideals he grew up with, was taught to respect and expected to defend. His is total treachery – the most sordid product of World War II.*

I think that is a revealing passage, showing profoundly the deep sense of personal betrayal that the radio propagandist draws from his or her audience. Even when the material sounds harmless or becomes ridiculous it can never be regarded as innocent.

This chapter was first delivered as 'Nation Shall Speak Unto Nation – or Words to that Effect' at the Welsh Centre for International Affairs on 30 October 1987.

WHAT'S DIFFERENT?
WHAT'S THE SAME? –
40 YEARS OF
EXTERNAL BROADCASTING

Each year in the autumn, the *BBC Annual Report and Handbook* used to land on our desks with a leaden thump. It cost £8 in 1986, it ran to 291 pages and it must have been one of the leading contenders for the nation's least-read public documents (though on reflection the challengers jostling for that title are numerous beyond belief). We shall not see its like again, unloved as it was. It has been killed in its old form and replaced by a style of report more in line with the new, more managerial, BBC.

At once this leviathan of a public document becomes interesting – it is part of a finite series of documents; it becomes history; it commemorates the BBC as it once was (I assume we are capable of change), an oganisation of Levantine complexity, of proliferating institutional support systems, of huge programme range, but with a perplexing lack of defined personality. As you skim the pages, for they defy reading, one question raises its voice: how did we arrive at this situation? I don't propose to answer that question for the BBC as a whole for such is not my responsibility. But I have been reflecting on how the External Services got to where they are today and my text has been those BBC Handbooks, or Yearbooks as they used to be called, that fill one shelf in my office.

Institutional writing is bland, protective, and designed to conceal, yet over the years the changes of approach and outlook show through most powerfully when they are least conscious. As I looked through the BBC Handbooks, I asked 'What's different? What's the same?' and I arrived at some surprising answers.

I should say first that I did not inflict on myself – and do not propose to try your patience with – a remorseless year by year review of how we have evolved. Rather like an archaeologist digging a trench through a great deal of debris, I have taken a dip into the External Services at a series of five-year intervals; or, to alter the metaphor, a family snapshot every five years.

I began with 1945, the last year of the wartime world, the first of the new era of peace. It was full of surprises. The frontispiece is of the French Foreign Minister, Georges Bidault, and his words set the tone of a document entirely about wartime broadcasting at home and abroad:

> *In this struggle of light against darkness, of truth against lies, the BBC for four years gave us the best and most effective weapons; it did not speak of an easy success, nor of unmerited glory; but it drew from the injustices of our misery a lesson of effort, courage and resistance. 'Ici Londres' . . . These were the words which, in the silence of occupation when every mouth was gagged, helped the French to surmount and overcome the lies of the enemy.*

Elsewhere there is a picture of Victor de Lavelye of the Belgian Service who it says was the originator of the most famous call sign in radio, the V-sign. And then no fewer than 46 pages – a third of the total – are devoted to the broadcasting effort overseas.

What's the same? A clear awareness that accurate news is the core of our *raison d'être*, and that information about Britain is an important part of the activity. But the relationship with the audience is very, very different.

In 1945 the needs of the Briton abroad were high on the list of priorities. As far back as 1929 the idea of what was called 'the lonely listener in the bush' helped to create a mental image of the listener at the receiving end. Others called them 'the lonely pioneers who are seeking something "beyond the ranges"' and one writer at the time imagined 'the men in the heart of an African desert hearing the frantic applause at a vaudeville item in the Palladium'.

In 1945 the Head of the BBC's Delhi office reflected on the conflicting needs of the British civilian and military audiences in India:

> *The soldier brings a determination NOT to be lulled by the tunes and ditties of pre-war days. He wants to be as up to date*

in his repertoire as anyone and if the catch-tunes of the day
happen to be poor – well, his taste is inherently sound, but he
is prepared to take the good with the bad, provided it's new.

I hope we are less patronising towards the audience today. Civilians in India were thought to like light music, the better-known classics, serious talks and what was called 'straight' dance music, whereas 'The Forces demand a lot of dance music, a little good "light" music, the minimum of spoken material. They like girl announcers; the civilians seem to detest them.' And how long it took to overcome that particular barrier.

Today expatriate listeners – though sometimes the most vocal in demanding a service tailored to their needs and one that reflects memories of a Britain that perhaps never existed – are not high on our list of priorities. Of the 25 million regular listeners to the World Service, the greatest proportion have English as a second language. That does not worry me – except technically. It means that we are reaching people who use us because we fill a need, a need quite as great as any ever experienced by the lonely listener in the bush.

Elsewhere the 1945 Handbook contains a piece on broadcasting to the United States. The North American Service had started in 1940, and by D-Day, in 1944, 725 out of 914 stations were rebroadcasting BBC reports. We produced special programmes for the networks: 'Transatlantic Call' for CBS; 'Atlantic Spotlight' for NBC; and 'Transatlantic Quiz' for the Blue Network. From 1943 a weekly 'London Column' was being transmitted on local stations to a potential 50 per cent of the total US audience. The report ended confidently: 'The bond of common language makes the future sharing of broadcast programmes between the British Commonwealth and the USA inevitable.'

Alas, such confidence was misplaced. Over the years, the pressures against such sharing of material increased. The switch to television, the commercialisation of American local radio stations, and a change of view in Britain about broadcasting to the United States ended the direct transatlantic flow of material. In fact the Foreign Office closed the North American Service. Broadcasting to allies was not regarded as a necessity. They – it was argued – were on our side anyway.

As a point of view this was short-sighted and complacent. It ignored the isolationist and parochial forces within the American media which would produce an American public opinion that was not hostile to Europe but something almost worse – profoundly ignorant. Americans would be so unaware of European politics, and so untutored in the common history of the last 40 years which underpinned the Atlantic Alliance, that the pattern of Anglo-American relations and the forces that shaped them would be simply unknown.

Today I argue, when I can, that the idea of broadcasting mainly to our enemies is one of the great heresies of external broadcasting. We cannot be simply in a position of opposition to our target areas. That would breed a combative, propagandist atmosphere which would rapidly undermine the credibility we enjoy as impartial distributors of news and information. We must talk to our friends as well and I am happy to say that our friends are listening. Without help from the government – or even any suggestion from them – we have found that there is an audience in the USA for our broadcasts and that the local radio networks have emerged from their previous narrow commercialism to an awareness that good accurate news is a commodity which a sizeable minority wants from its local FM stations.

We now enjoy an estimated audience of two million in the USA on short wave alone, and our agreement with the more than 400 stations of the American Public Radio network – over 70 of whom relay our programmes – gives us an entrée to the homes of some millions more. A man must find time to keep his friendships in good repair – so must a nation find time to talk to its allies and not take them for granted. I hope that the dashed hopes of 1945 *vis-à-vis* links with the United States are now being revived in a new and more appropriate form for the times.

In the 1950 Yearbook, under a section headed 'Other Countries', the writer states: 'American excitement over television has not seriously affected BBC rebroadcasting in the United States.' In that sentence you can hear the fastidious distancing of the writer from the new – and supposedly transitory – joys of new-fangled television. Yet are we making the same mistakes now over cable and satellite transmissions?

What else did 1950 bring? A historic event on 3 April 1949 –

separate transmissions for India and Pakistan in recognition of
the separate existence of the two new states. They became separate linguistic entities too. Instead of a single Hindustani Service
covering the land of the Raj, there was now an Urdu Service for
Pakistan and a Hindi Service for India. They were modest begin-
nings: for Hindi, a half-hour daily programme with two news bulletins; for Urdu a half-hour programme followed by 15 minutes of
news and current affairs.

And today? The Hindi Service now broadcasts for 2 hours a day,
reaching (according to a 1981 survey) no fewer than 35 million
adults in the whole of India. It is a staggering audience. When the
figures first appeared no one believed them. Over the years we
have come to see that they did indeed identify a huge reservoir of
listeners of a kind that even the optimists had not believed
existed. The Urdu Service broadcasts for some 1½ hours a day,
reaching ten million in India and five million in Pakistan. At
times of crisis these figures almost certainly rise. That is not surprising given the control exercised over the electronic media in
India (by contrast with the freedom and quality of the Indian
press). Rajiv Gandhi had to tune in to the BBC World Service to
hear of his mother's assassination while All India Radio debated
how and when to carry the news – such is the climate within
which Indians tune into a foreign radio station to satisfy their
need for news information.

Does it matter? There is a school of thought which says that the
External Services should talk to opinion-formers only. Who
influences decisions? Who shapes policy? One Prime Minister is
worth a million farmers, you might say. It is a dangerous view and
in my opinion represents the second great heresy of external
broadcasting: that the select few matter more than the
undifferentiated many. For a start it turns the medium on its
head. It is not narrowcasting, it is broadcasting. Further, such a
view would ascribe to narrowcasting an accuracy and precise targeting that it is simply not capable of. Thirdly, it reveals a simplistic view of opinion-formation that is not borne out by events.
Even leaders do not shape their decisions in isolation from the
societies they govern. The inclinations and aspirations of the
ruled have an impact on the acts of the rulers. Finally, the proposition that a mass audience is insignificant is clearly nonsensical,

especially when we imagine that same audience being addressed by another power.

Supposing we did not have an audience of 35 million Hindi speakers but Radio Moscow, or Radio Peking or even Voice of America did. Would we regard that as insignificant? Or would we react with alarm to a situation where masses of Indians were exposed to a world view which is so at odds with our own? I think in such a situation we would feel that the BBC External Services were falling down on their job and not talking to the people they should be. The fact that we can talk to mass audiences in Hindi, Urdu and Bengali, Tamil and Pashto goes back in part to that early decision in 1949.

In 1955 the Yearbook has become a Handbook. There is a functional feel to it. There are no pictures, glossy or otherwise. But there is some meat to the publication, some of those definitions of principle that make up the operational beliefs that sustain us on a day-to-day basis today. The Handbook quotes the then Director of External Broadcasting, Sir Ian Jacob. He defined the basic aims of the External Services as follows:

> *To state the truth with as much exactitude and sincerity as it is given to human beings to achieve; to elucidate objectively the world situation and the thoughts and actions of this country; and to build a closer understanding between peoples by providing interesting information and entertainment each in due measure according to the needs of the many audiences.*

I think that is well put. I like the confident commitment to truth – no hint of relativity there – no weasel qualifications. The view of what is possible in the world through communication is a simpler one than anything we could entertain today. But the essential position is outlined, the posture of independence established.

By 1955 too, the Handbook can quote the words of the Government White Paper on Broadcasting, setting out a fundamental tenet of broadcasting policy:

> *The Government intend that the Corporation should remain independent in the preparation of programmes for overseas audiences, though it should obtain from the Government Departments concerned, such information about conditions in*

these countries, and the policies of HM Government towards them, as will permit it to plan the programmes in the national interest.

I think there was a noose hanging there, carefully but nonchalantly dangled by a civil servant. Would broadcasters adopt the world view of diplomats by being so regularly exposed to their assessments of countries? The danger must have been there. In my experience, as the years have gone by, the principles of journalism, rather than the values and priorities of diplomacy, have become the directing principles of the External Services. Certainly by the time I first set foot in the External Services in 1960, I knew that I was part of a journalistic organisation and not a part of the Foreign Office. I do not know how surefooted my predecessors had to be between then and 1955 to chart their independence through this narrow passage but they did so with a clear instinct from which we benefit today.

I turned to the 1960 Handbook with a special personal interest. This was the official account of the organisation I joined when I started my first job. Would I recognise in its terse narration anything of the spirit that made me and scores of others want to work in this area of broadcasting? Not really. The frontispiece carries the then Chairman, Sir Arthur Fforde, and the Director-General, Sir Ian Jacob. They seemed – they were – shadowy and remote figures to us then. Are we, at the top levels of management, any more shadowy, remote and – dare I say it – irrelevant to the daily work of a busy producer than those considerable men were to us? I can't answer that.

I do note that the book refers to the department that I joined – Overseas Talks and Features – as the department originating feature programmes on current events for the then General Overseas Service. It's worth taking a moment to think about what was seen then as current affairs. And remember that we weren't behind the domestic services in our coverage, rather that all current affairs were in a very rudimentary state in 1960.

The department had just started a revolutionary idea: a daily 15-minute news feature called *The World Today*, concentrating on one subject each day. There were many objections to this idea: in particular, that there weren't enough subjects around to warrant one topic each day; and even if there were, it was very unlikely that you could fill 15 minutes on each one. *Sancta Simplicitas.* Twenty-nine years later *The World Today* still exists, finding subjects and an ever-widening range of speakers with effortless ease.

In programmes such as *24 Hours, Newsdesk, Commentary*, a range of other specialist news programmes were only glimpsed darkly in the 1960s, to be built on subsequently. In 1960 the World Service was a 22-hour-a-day service; now it broadcasts round the clock.

By 1965 the Handbook has become a paperback, price 7 shillings and sixpence. The style, design and rather abstract cover point to a determination to be modern. Inside, the pages on the External Services reveal a harder-edged and distinctly modern world. We are no longer in the post-war era but one in which the outlines of the opportunities and problems we face today are becoming clear. It's the start of the modern age in another sense. The cover picture is of Robin Day, Hugh Greene and Lord Normanbrook, the Chairman, musing on the set of the 1964 General Election. All three are authentic giants of the modern broadcasting world.

For the External Services, it was good news and bad news. The number of radio sets in the world had risen from 150 million just after the war to 434 million. They represented a huge opportunity and a new audience. On the other hand, that audience was increasingly tempted by the growing power and availability of television – 138 million sets – and our ability to reach the new audience, whether distracted by television or not, was limited by the shortage of overseas relay stations. We had just two – Singapore and Ascension Island – while the Americans already had 15. And we had begun to slide inexorably down the world ladder of hours broadcast. We were now fourth after the Soviet Union, China and Voice of America, with West Germany creeping up steadily. And 24 years later we are fifth – after the Federal Republic – even though our weekly broadcast hours have risen from 620 to 733.

In another sense 1965 was a watershed year. Rebroadcasting by national broadcasting stations was still a sizeable phenomenon. The Handbook contains a two-page list of countries, from Angola to Zambia, where there was direct broadcasting of either the

General Overseas Service (GOS) or a vernacular service. Of the 70 countries who broadcast transmissions, over three-quarters carried a daily rebroadcast. It was an impressive performance, essentially a relic of the post-war and colonial periods. In the full flush of nationalism most of those countries would conclude that they should not receive the news programmes, the world view, of another power, especially one associated with a colonial past. Interestingly, nearly a quarter of a century on, there are now signs of a new readiness to rebroadcast our programmes directly, simply because we offer a news service recognised as better than that of others.

On to 1970, and another feature of the modern world: the government inquiry, the first of many such over the last 15 years. In fact the External Services had been subjected to review at an average rate of one every three years but that of Sir Val Duncan was something radical. As the writer of the Handbook observed, Duncan's single chapter was based 'on very little examination of broadcasters, broadcasts or those who listen to broadcasts'. Its conclusions though were confident. I paraphrase them without, I hope, parodying them: Britain's information effort abroad should switch overall from policy presentation to commercial and cultural promotion; broadcasting should be directed to the 'influential few'; and since those influential few clearly spoke English then, apart from the Middle East and Eastern Europe, all the vernacular services should be abolished. The 1970 Handbook eloquently defended the practice of vernacular broadcasting:

> *There is no special magic in the fact that 40 languages are used to permeate the world with BBC broadcasts. But there is magic in ensuring that most people in the world can listen in a language they can really understand and that whatever the language or destination, all services are evidently based on the same principles.*

Duncan disappeared without trace, a heretic of too single-minded and too skewed a vision, looking for a simple answer to a complex problem.

One other feature of 1970 – a long search was starting for reliable audience figures. At this point any idea of audience size was mainly derived from letters and answers to questionnaires. Today we are told that letters are no guide to the size of the audience. But here and there we are starting to pinpoint the number of people who did bother to tune in.

In 1975, another buzz word of the decade is first heard – 'cuts'. There was indeed a financial crisis – and the External Services had to make their share of savings – £390 000 off current expenditure and the deferment of the capital programme to yield another £540 000. The Handbook warned:

> *These cuts must be seen in the context of the statement made in last year's report that continued deferment of capital expenditure and the pressure of repeated economies in the field of programme expenditure were seriously damaging in the increasingly competitive world in which External Broadcasting operates.*

There is little point in moaning about government spending cuts or trying to enter a case of special pleading. But we all feel the thorn in our shoe and this one was the first of many successive thorns which hurt. Furthermore, these cuts – above all the delays imposed on a modest capital programme – took place in an atmosphere where our rivals were investing heavily in an activity which we had, in some senses, made our own. The transmitter deficit – our version of the missile gap – would surface dramatically before the end of the decade.

The Handbook for 1980 highlights two developments which colour our activities to this day. In the context of the need to resist calls for a so-called 'New World Information Order', the writer warned of the application of the ideology behind this movement to the frequencies on which we broadcast; equal shares for all, regardless of the existing situation. The threat from the World Administrative Radio Conference (WARC) repeated itself in 1980, in the shape of a proposal so to regulate and allocate the short-wave frequencies that all should have equal access to them, the demand regulated by a computer-based plan run from Geneva. The 1987 WARC then agreed to defer any such proposal until a later conference which would examine whether this type of computer plan could actually do the desired job.

More positively, 1980 recorded the start of a ten-year modernisation programme which put more capital into our overseas relay stations than we have ever had before. The reality was that External Services audibility had reached a critical point, almost one of no return. Nearing the end of that programme, it is good to be able to report that it has kept us in the big league, though the competition may be about to outstrip us decisively.

And the 1980 Handbook puts a figure on the audience – 75 million adults who listened to the output at least once a week. The External Services had moved into the modern age.

By 1985, the outlines of the environment that we live in today are well established. Competition by our rivals, such as the Voice of America, has taken on a more determined form with a huge capital programme of transmitter development running at a massive £87 million in that year alone. The threat from the string of American 'super-relay' stations composed entirely of 500 kW transmitters is still to appear on the air waves. It should not be underestimated, especially as the BBC and the Foreign & Commonwealth Office examine the next stages of capital development.

But the 1985 Handbook recorded two domestic developments which are still relevant today. First, that Bush House 'inevitably feels some frustration at being held within the limit of the existing hours and the number of transmissions'. Those frustrations have been somewhat relaxed as the hours broadcast have moved steadily upwards, without extra funding, from 733 hours per week in 1986 to more than 772 in 1990. Such a marked improvement in productivity also enables us to respond to new broadcasting opportunities as they occur. Secondly, the Handbook notes that, 'Ministers and officials have continued to stress the value they place on the operation of the External Services'. If there is a faint undertone of fine words buttering no broadcasting parsnips, then it is only just detectable.

Elsewhere, the foundations are being laid for the major developments of the last years – the 648 metres Medium Wave transmitter at Orfordness in Suffolk opened – without it the trilingual frequency which represents Britain in North-west Europe, BBC 648, could not have been born as it was in 1987. Negotiations on relay stations in Hong Kong and Seychelles 'made good progress'. In fact, Hong Kong's opened in 1987, the Seychelles' in 1988. Without the former, World Service would not have played the extraordinary role that it did during the Tienanmen Square democracy movement in China in 1989, nor would the BBC voice be growing as it is in East Africa without the extra audibility generated from the Seychelles. In short, the 1985 Handbook is a reassuring one to read, setting out as it does a path of steady and successful progress. We are recognisably in the world we now inhabit.

What will the 1990 Report to Parliament highlight? Steady increases in productivity; some dramatic breakthroughs in rebroadcasting World Service output on the domestic networks of countries – such as Poland – where the very notion would have been inconceivable even two years ago; continued consolidation of audiences and impact on a broad front. It will also record the strikes of 1989, a danger signal that the World Service needs the best staff to do its work but is unable to match the pay offered in the rest of the domestic media.

One aspect will be too familiar. The expressions of official approval for World Service's activities will continue. But so will the sound of an organisation severely stretched and about to be stretched dangerously by the impact of outside competition. For almost 60 years, the World Service and its funding has muddled through. 1990 may also record that for the first time the World Service has charted its desired course for the next decade. That will be a real landmark.

This chapter was first delivered as 'What's Different? What's the Same? – Looking back over 40 Years of External Broadcasting' at Oxford University's Alastair Buchan Club on 12 March 1987.

II

THE BBC AROUND THE WORLD

THE LATIN
AMERICAN SERVICES
AFTER 50 YEARS

The Spanish and Portuguese Services of the BBC began their existence in March 1938, more than 50 years ago. What I propose to do is to examine some of the key experiences of the last half-century of broadcasting to Latin America before considering where we stand today and where we and the Services should be going. The issues facing these Services, and the principles according to which they work, also throw light on the workings of External Broadcasting as a whole.

During the 1930s, the regimes which first realised the value and potential of the new medium of short-wave broadcasting were the dictatorships – both Fascist and Communist. The democracies, often held back by their scruples, took longer to realise that the competition for the ears and minds of the world was being won by our enemies. The Germans set their sights on Latin America from the early days of foreign broadcasting and, in particular, pioneered the rebroadcasting of their programmes on the airwaves of local radio stations. German transmissions began three years ahead of ours, in 1935, and made no attempt to conceal their political message, including attacks on what they called 'dollar diplomacy' and 'Yankee Imperialism'. Those direct German broadcasts were reinforced by local rebroadcasting which totalled almost 500 programmes in 1937 (a year when the number of British tapes rebroadcast in the continent could be, and was, counted on the fingers of one hand).

How did Britain respond? It had taken the Director-General, John Reith, five years to persuade the government that international broadcasting was worth doing at all, in any language. Perhaps it is truer to say that its value was recognised but no one was prepared to pay the price. Reith was finally told that the BBC could go ahead and pay for the project itself if it was so convinced of its importance, and he did so in December 1932.

The question of broadcasting in languages other than English posed a further problem. Was it right? From the very beginning there was disagreement on this subject between the BBC and the government, with the BBC expressing doubts as to whether broadcasting in languages other than English would not distort the purity and disinterested nature of the message, and would not be seen and become propaganda? As late as 1936, when German and Italian radio propaganda was having a major and damaging impact in the Middle East and Latin America, Reith – reflecting his colleagues' anxieties – noted:

> *It is more in Britain's interest – and also a subtle form of propaganda from the British point of view – to avoid any action that might lead listeners, who have turned to British bulletins as a reliable source of information, to think that we too were joining in the babble of broadcast nationalist propaganda.*

It was a babble associated with broadcasting in other languages. As late as 1939 Cecil Graves, the first Director of the Empire Services, voiced his anxiety that broadcasting in German might lead to reprisals and what he called 'German listeners feeling that we were propaganding' (*sic*). (At that time we didn't even have a proper word for it.)

The Ullswater Committee of 1936 gave considerable impetus to vernacular broadcasting by recommending in its favour. And the frequently voiced anxieties of the British Embassies in the region no doubt added to this impetus. In 1937 Felix Greene, then the BBC's representative in New York, was ordered to tour Latin America and report his findings. He recorded how, as he put it: 'Countless Brazilians, Argentinians and Chileans have told me how difficult it is to stand by and lift no finger to protect Britain's name and interests'. And he noted: 'We are facing damaging propaganda in all its forms, propaganda concerted, skilful, highly organised and prosecuted with resourcefulness, energy and infinite diligence'. That may be a somewhat excessive description of what was probably by our standards a pretty rudimentary broadcasting system but I am sure that it faithfully reflects the anxieties which the wholly new medium of external broadcasting, especially in its propagandistic form, was stirring up.

After much further debate Reith agreed to start broadcasts in Arabic, Spanish and Portuguese on six conditions, some of whose terms are still valid today. If foreign language broadcasts were to be transmitted from Britain, then they must be done by the BBC; they must be on a considerable scale; they must include both news and what Reith called 'sustaining programmes' (ie, of general interest); they needed extra finance; and the BBC should be as editorially independent in these broadcasts as in its home services. We would stand by all those conditions today. Only one of Reith's conditions is, I believe, not valid today, namely that 'foreign language services must not prejudice the Empire Service'. Today we at Bush House know very well that, as Chairman Mao might have said, but did not, 'International broadcasting marches on two legs.'

We need, and Britain needs, both the English and the vernacular services to be truly effective. The vernacular broadcasts get larger audiences; they create and appeal to mass audiences; they reach the audience more directly and powerfully because they transcend the language barrier; and they provide both news of the world and news of the country concerned. They are a vital complement to the more universal, more global World Service. To me this seems self-evident. Experience has shown that it is so. Regrettably, there are still people in influential positions who regard the vernaculars as services which continually have to prove their worth because their worth cannot be taken for granted. It is an attitude that we attempt constantly to correct.

So, on the memorable night of 14–15 March, more than 50 years ago, what was the programme with which Britain and the BBC began to turn back the relentless tide of Hunnish distortion? What was the cultural contribution that we offered to persuade doubting Latin Americans that there was a better, democratic, western way? Why, 35 minutes of dance music from the Piccadilly Hotel, London, by Maurice Winnick and his Orchestra. After news in English – because the services interleaved with one another awkwardly for many years – more music from the resoundingly named BBC Empire Orchestra, Conductor Eric Fogg, and Harriet Cohen at the Pianoforte. At 1.26 pm GMT there was a special added news item, though history does not record why it was so listed: 'British Farmers and Chilled Beef

Competition' by Anthony Hurd – father of the present Foreign Secretary.

It is always easy to poke fun at the programme listings of yesterday, but what matters is the purpose behind the programmes and their effectiveness. Lord Winterton told the House of Lords 'Our moderation and the reliability of the British word' are generally recognised. A BBC official promised 'straight objective news bulletins'. On the morning after, the *Evening Standard* reported from Montevideo somewhat dismally (but the words have an all too familiar ring): 'Reception of the music was indifferent, but the news was heard clearly.' And so it is, all too often today, though I believe that both get through far better than ever before as the ten-year audibility programme of transmitter improvements and expansion starts to have its effect.

The Latin American Service's wartime growth and impact were spectacular, providing 5¾ hours per day of Spanish and 4 of Brazilian in November 1943. In the same year 100 stations were rebroadcasting us on medium wave every day, leading in the post-war period to a possibly unique degree of cultural co-operation between Britain and the continent. Major dramas such as *Don Quijote* and *Cristobal Colon* were produced in London using actors flown in from Madrid, with specially commissioned music by Manuel Lazareno, performed by the Hallé Orchestra and Sir Malcolm Sargent. I am told that, to this day, the discs containing such radio classics are still kept and proudly displayed by their possessors to BBC visitors. It is an archive not to be taken for granted or underestimated.

In the post-war period, although the Ministry of Information declared the Latin American Service to be 'the most far-reaching means of presenting the British case, our ideals and our way of life and thought', these were the hard years, of austerity, of paying the costs of a war we could not afford. In 1951 the Service was heavily cut and since then it has always had to argue its case with government twice as hard as any other service.

We approached the nadir with the publication of the Duncan Report on Britain's Overseas Representation in 1969. It recommended swingeing cuts in vernacular services especially Latin America, because, to quote its briskly straightforward argument: 'Latin America was not an area in which British interests were involved to such a major degree.' The attitude displayed by Sir Val Duncan and his colleagues bore one bitter fruit in 1981 when Spanish was cut altogether – though Spanish for Latin America was spared – and Brazilian was reprieved from extinction but reduced by 1¾ hours.

The reduction in the Brazilian Service and the elimination of Spanish took effect on 31 March 1982. Two days later, on 2 April 1982, Argentine forces occupied Port Stanley. Within days the BBC was asked to expand its transmissions in Spanish for Latin America. It was assumed that the Brazilian cuts would be restored too, given the pivotal position of Brazil in the delicate diplomacy surrounding the Falklands. Regrettably, this was one U-turn too many for officials and politicians to take. The Brazilian output remained cut.

Nothing could have pointed up more cruelly the short-sighted nature of the cuts exercise than the Falklands War. It should have been a conclusive reminder that diplomats are not as omniscient as they sometimes claim to be, that international relations is an uncertain art and that the point of insurance is to have a policy in operation before the fire breaks out. And vernacular broadcasting services are – in at least one respect – an insurance policy.

It is worth pointing out too that although the Spanish American transmission was increased in the Falklands emergency from 4 to 5½ hours a day, by the time the war ended ten weeks later, the extra staff needed for such a prescription increase had not been recruited and trained. They could not have been – it is not like turning on a tap. Who produced and voiced the extra programming? Who else but the existing staff, already demoralised, buffeted and undermined by cuts, threats of extinction and a constant barrage of official doubts about their usefulness. Those existing professional staff worked day and night during the war because it was their professional duty and because they had the professional skill to do so. Such skill and devotion should not be taken for granted and cannot be found at a moment's notice.

The Falklands War put BBC principles throughout the Corporation to the test. I was working on *Newsnight* at the time and we acted on the basic journalistic assumption that all claims – from whatever source – had to be tested for veracity, even at the risk of being charged by the self-styled super-patriots with treason. It was very noticeable that as the war progressed, the military bulletins from Buenos Aires became more, not less, reliable. As they did, so the Ministry of Defence in London had to modify its own responses. On occasion the news of British losses – accurate news, too – came first from Argentina and second only from London. In allowing this to happen, the Defence Ministry ignored the lesson learned during the Second World War by BBC newsmen that when a British battleship was sunk or a battle lost, then the very first news of that disaster *had* to come from London. During the Falklands, it often did not.

By pursuing no doubt similar principles, the Latin American Service proved yet again that in war truth does not need to be the first casualty. In fact it is often the great survivor. Increasingly, Argentinians learned that the BBC told the truth even while Britain undertook a military gamble which probably most of the world thought she would lose. On 17 April, a cartoon in *La Prensa* showed a small boy whispering to a man in the street: 'Psst, Señor – Que dice la BBC?' A letter from a young Argentine told us how he bravely took his radio with him to his hospital ward in order to listen to the BBC Spanish Service. This was not a popular act. Many called him 'traitor'. By the time the Task Force troops had reached Goose Green, the entire ward was gathering regularly to listen to the news from Bush House.

It is more than a footnote to history that the Service played a direct part in the final moments before surrender. Padre Salvatore Santore, Argentine Military Chaplain on the islands, told the *Yorkshire Post* on 6 July that once General Menendez, the Argentine Military Commander, heard through the BBC Spanish Service that the war was in its terminal stages, he disregarded orders from Buenos Aires to fight on.

During a Foreign Affairs Committee inquiry last year a Conservative MP told me that a listener in the Caribbean commented to him on the BBC's coverage during the war. 'You couldn't tell whose side they were on,' he observed with approval.

Well, memories are short. You would not think from the comments of some officials or the observations of ambassadors that the Spanish and Portuguese Services had performed such a signal service to the nation so recently. You would think that they were an expensive and dispensable luxury whose justification required a considerable act of faith. There are 49 people in the entire Latin American Service. They broadcast 40 hours a week – 31 in Spanish, 9 in Brazilian – and the cost is £1.3 million: £1.3 million to talk to a continent of 390 million people whose importance can do nothing but grow.

How large are the audiences? The only figures we have are for the audiences who listen to our direct broadcasts regularly on short wave. They are not large; they are not television-sized; but should they be dismissed just because of that? Out of only nine countries surveyed in the continent, the total *regular* audience in urban areas is some 1¼ million people. So for just £1 per person per year, Britain has regular communication with these people, and their numbers swell during a crisis, as the doubling of the audience in Argentina during the Falklands War demonstrated. In some countries we are the largest external broadcaster; in others we are second only to Voice of America; in all we are the most respected.

But there is a further audience which is hard for diplomats to discern or for our audience research to measure – the audience which listens to BBC news material rebroadcast on local radio stations. The Latin American Services are developing inroads into this new market. Every week the Spanish Service sends a disc containing four 15-minute programmes to 368 radio stations. The Portuguese Service sends 30 cassettes a week containing 4–5 programmes. We believe the usage of these discs is high. In addition, a daily 5-minute international current affairs package is sent by satellite to seven major regional network centres and broadcast immediately on arrival.

We can't count the listeners to these indirect broadcasts although we want to do so. We can only guess at their impact, though we ought nevertheless to be able to imagine it. And they should certainly weigh more heavily in any calculation, subjective or objective, of the value of the service.

Yet the entire argument about the size and value of the audience in Latin America runs on mistaken lines. Just what is a large or a small audience? Take the evidence from Honduras. A 1989 survey estimates the audience for the BBC Spanish Service as between 25 000 and 30 000 adults. Such figures seem small but they are in fact rather extraordinary. The population of that small

Central American state is just 2.5 million. A regular audience of 25–30 000 must represent the equivalent of the circulation of a small evening paper. Supposing Honduras enjoyed a British-run and -edited paper of such a size, that would be rightly regarded as a significant element in relations between the two countries. Since the audience is delivered at zero marginal extra cost and effort – the transmitters are already transmitting, the programmes are made – what might appear a tiny audience becomes in reality pretty good value for money.

Since this question of impact and value for money is constantly raised, and understandably so, here are a few comparisons.

Firstly, as I noted earlier, £1 allows Britain to speak to one person for a whole year, on a regular daily basis if that person wishes. You cannot reach an individual for that sort of money by any other method. You could send him or her a postcard by airmail – one solitary card – each year. You could invite him or her to one diplomatic gathering but you wouldn't be able to offer more than a glass of wine and a sausage roll. And in many provincial capitals there are no diplomats to pass round the wine and rolls. To coin a phrase, short-wave broadcasts reach the parts and people that diplomats cannot reach.

Secondly, for £1 million a year, you cannot speak to people in all of Latin America's 19 nations by any other means. You could not reach them by local radio; you could not run a newspaper. You could not buy many advertisements. This is the only way you can talk to people, the educated people, the often politically vital middle class, the lawyers, the doctors and students and teachers. It is the role of the diplomats to talk to the relatively small numbers of high-level opinion-makers. If you want the ear of the President, ask the Ambassador to phone.

Thirdly, for £1 million a year you both conduct a continuing dialogue and maintain an emergency service which can respond to the unforeseen crisis. That insurance policy for Spanish-speaking Latin America costs just £600 000 a year. After the Falklands War, who can say it will not be needed? Who can argue that it was not value for money?

Fourthly, because the Latin American Service has been broadcasting for over 50 years and because it comes from the BBC, it is believed. For £1 million you are marketing and projecting credibility, and a credibility which redounds to Britain's credit.

Lastly, after 50 years on the air, after the shared experiences of peace and war, with direct broadcasts reinforced by a growing pattern of indirect broadcasting where there is a clear demand for the BBC and British product, anyone who contemplates radical cuts on the basis of the limited and uncertain evidence we possess is taking the most blatant leap in the dark. Quite simply, they would not know what they were proposing to destroy and, as we have discovered in the past, it is only when a service is cut that the full extent of its hold is revealed, and the damage done.

So finally I come back to the Falklands. It is not conceded often enough – especially by critics of the Falklands campaign – that its greatest and most beneficial consequence was the restoration of democracy in Argentina. The great lesson of the Falklands conflict as far as international broadcasting is concerned is that there is no substitute for having an existing, well-organised, professional base when the crisis comes. After all, who would have expected trouble in that part of the world at that particular time? But the audience was there, though small to start with. Despite jamming by the Argentine authorities the audience grew. And despite the commandeering of a BBC transmitter on Ascension Island by the Ministry of Defence to set up the Ministry station, 'Radio Atlantico del Sur', it was the BBC that people turned to, not the strange and suspect voice of the government.

As John Reith said back in 1937 when the vernacular services were being set up, it is important for the BBC to remain distinct from government. And as he wrote in his autobiography: 'The BBC would be trusted, where the government might not be.' The case of the Falklands is just one of many which has proved him right.

This chapter was first delivered as 'The Latin American Service of the BBC' at the Canning Club on 24 February 1988.

BROADCASTING AFTER GLASNOST

In November 1987 the BBC Russian Service's regular disc jockey Sam Yossman ended his regular selection of old pop favourites, *Granny's Chest*, and waited to see if the audience would respond. To be frank, the number of phone calls in reply to Sam's programme had been disappointing to date. But that day, 27 November, something happened. Over the next 4 hours, 72 phone calls poured in from all over the Soviet Union. They came from Alma-Ata in the south to Archangel in the north. At one stage the Leningrad operator cried out, 'Don't hang up Sam, I've got four more people queuing up here who want to speak to you.' These calls had to be made from public post offices. They cost 3 roubles (£3 at the official exchange rate) per minute. Yet they came in unprecedented numbers. Such calls have now become a regular feature of our contact with the audience in the Soviet Union. In January this year the Russian Service received a further 194 calls, suggesting that there has been a change of some kind in the Soviet Union under *glasnost*. How far it would go and how long it would last are questions which require constant enquiry and vigilant scepticism.

The Russians are not the only members of the Soviet bloc with whom we now have regular telephone contact. The BBC Bulgarian Service pioneered these telephone calls as long ago as January 1987. In the previous year, the section had received just 60 letters and even that was high in comparison with earlier years. Was there anybody out there at all? Since the phone line was opened, we now know that there was and there is. In February 1988 alone, the Section received 290 phone calls. That figure may be on the low side in reflecting the number of callers. Many ring off when they find themselves connected to an ansaphone during off-duty hours. But many of those who do talk to our Bulgarian Section say they are calling from the office since such calls cannot be traced as easily as international calls made from a private phone.

I would not like you to think that there has been any generalised opening throughout the Eastern bloc. In Romania, phone calls, like almost everything else, are strictly rationed. Each Romanian citizen does have the right to call abroad – but only four times per year and then the charge for each extra call climbs to a prohibitive price. Each of those four calls has to be booked in advance. Understandably, very, very few run the risk of booking even one of their phone calls to the BBC in London. Severe as this restriction on personal communication may seem, it is comparatively light in comparison with the celebrated, or notorious, Romanian typewriter law, which demands that every typewriter in private hands be registered with the security authorities. *Glasnost* does not reign in an unchallenged way throughout the socialist camp and even in the Soviet Union there is a severe practical limitation – you can be open about anything so long as you do not challenge *glasnost* itself or *perestroika* and, of course, Soviet foreign policy. They are the key elements of the new party line – a more open, accessible one, and one which offers positive possibilities.

New openings have also become available to us as broadcasters in the BBC External Services. In the last two or so years the environment in which all our Eastern bloc services broadcast has changed to some extent. The two major openings, though, have been in our Russian and Polish Services, where jamming was finally lifted. The Russian jamming came off on 21 January 1987, the Polish on 1 January 1988. Let me deal with the Russian Service first, and then the Polish.

The pattern of jamming of our Russian Service has been a broadly cyclical one over the last 30 years. It first came on in 1949, and was lifted briefly in 1956. It was lifted again in the early sixties, between 1963 and 1968 but restored on the night of the Soviet-led invasion of Czechoslovakia. Jamming was lifted again between 1973 and August 1980, when events in Poland were at their most dramatic and it was reimposed until the present lifting.

Three things should be noted. Firstly, jamming is extremely expensive. Two years ago BBC engineers calculated that the annual cost of jamming by the Soviet Union was in the region of

$800 million, because the jammer has to transmit a blocking noise as strong as the incoming signal. Although skywave jamming (which covered large areas) returned in 1981, local jamming concentrated on urban conurbations which meant that audibility was better in the country areas. Secondly, despite jamming, some signal does get through. To give listeners the best chance of hearing our programmes we ran a heavy pattern of repeats. Because of human perversity, the worse the jamming, the greater the determination to hear something through the clatter and mush. Despite jamming, the BBC Russian Service had an audience and a good one. According to the only available figures – research we share with the American stations Radio Free Europe and Radio Liberty – our audience during jamming was of the order of some 14 million listeners a week. Thirdly, jamming was reserved for the output of the Russian Service. The BBC World Service, broadcasting around the world 24 hours a day in English, was not jammed. I will suggest an explanation for such an apparently contradictory response a little later.

The response of the BBC Russian Service to the end of jamming has been at several levels. Firstly, the number of repeats has been reduced – each feature programme was repeated twice under jamming; now each one is repeated once only in the course of the 6¾ hours per day that the Russian Service broadcasts. As a result, the Russian listener can tune in to a continuous run of 5½ hours of broadcasting each evening without hearing the same programme twice. Secondly, with more room for news and analysis, a new programme has been introduced called *Argument* – or *Discussion* – which covers current affairs in a more lively, discursive and interview-oriented way that is proving popular with listeners. Although *Argument* only went on the air last September a majority of our 194 phone calls in January named it as interesting and valuable. One caller from the town of Vladimir praised *Argument* for what he called its 'philosophical approach to world problems and its higher professional standards'. Thirdly, the Russian Service now plans to restyle its other main current affairs programme *London View*. Fourthly, the departments which provide written analysis of international events around the world for the entire External Services have restyled their output by shortening their reports from 65 lines – or 600 words – to a more immediate, more usable 400 to 500 words. In view of all this, it was encouraging to read the comment of one caller that 'after the *perestroika* in the Russian Service of the BBC, one hardly bothers to listen to any other station' – not wholly true but nice that someone said it.

Since the end of jamming, the audience for the BBC Russian Service appears to have risen. For a time we enjoyed the privilege of unjammed audibility while our main competitors, Voice of America (VOA) and Deutsche Welle, still suffered interference. The audience rose sharply; the sheer relief of being able to hear clearly helped. Our superior competitive position helped too; and the hunger of Soviet citizens for free and accurate information in those early months of *glasnost* was particularly acute. Since jamming has since been lifted from VOA and Deutsche Welle, we have lost that initial gain. But the figures suggest – and we must be cautious about them – that the BBC Russian Service's total audience stands at around seven million who listen each day, 16 million who listen each week, and over 17 million who listen each month. And the Soviet authorities are aware of the scale and impact of this listening.

For example, there were the allegations in *Pravda* in 1988 that foreign stations, including the BBC and VOA, were instigating and inciting unrest in Armenia and Azerbaijan. The best way to deny those charges is to tell you a little of the approach of our Russian Service to the reporting of these events. First, did we inflate the death toll? At a time when the death toll was officially stated to be two, the BBC Russian Service carried an interview with Mrs Grigoryants, wife of a well-known dissident publisher, giving 17 as the likely death toll. Shortly after that claim, the official Soviet spokesman admitted to 32 deaths. We stuck to the figure of 32.

We also reported that unofficial estimates put the death toll at several hundred. The source was again Mrs Grigoryants who had on the earlier occasion proved herself a reliable, even somewhat cautious source. She claimed that it was 'definitely known' that 200 bodies had been buried. The Russian Service also established from *Pravda*'s American correspondent, Ovcharyenko, that some people in Sumgait were reported to be 'missing'. Later Mrs Grigoryants confirmed that several lists of missing people were circulating, with no duplication among the names. Together these lists added up to three figures. In these circumstances it was admissible to report the fact that far higher unofficial death estimates were circulating while continuing to report the official figure.

Throughout this time the Russian Service attempted to speak to official spokesmen and government sources in the Soviet Union, usually without success. We did broadcast an interview with *Pravda*'s Ovcharyenko, after three days of incessant telephoning. We did broadcast an interview with the Deputy Editor of the Party paper in Stepanarkert (the capital of the disputed enclave of Nagorny Karabakh) who accused *Pravda* of writing lies. We repeatedly attempted to contact Party officials and newspapers in Azerbaijan because we wanted to reflect their point of view as well as that of people who might be dismissed as Armenian dissidents or nationalists.

We have no interest in excluding the official view but our experience has been that unofficial sources have been repeatedly confirmed in their estimates by official spokesmen after the event. We will continue to attempt to establish from all sources the true extent and nature of such events, and we will keep on phoning – it would be nice if some phones in the Soviet Union were lifted rather more freely and openly. I might add that when Boris Yeltsin was sacked as Party Chief in Moscow, we tried to phone him to get his reaction – we did not get it, but we were right to try.

The Russian Service is our second largest foreign language service. With a staff of 50 it costs £1 200 000: just over £1 million is accounted for by staff costs. That leaves an exiguous £125 000 per annum for programme costs, which amounts to £2500 per week or just over £54 per hour of programme output. You may regard that as a low sum. I certainly do. In the increasingly competitive field of international broadcasting three factors determine the size of the audience: How loud is your signal? How credible are your values? How good are your programmes?

While the constant feedback from our audience praises the BBC's objectivity (clearly an essential commodity as far as the listeners are concerned) and this suggests that our values are right, we have always lagged behind in transmitter power. We cannot ignore programme quality either, though there is a tendency in some quarters to argue that if we get such a large and appreciative audience with such small resources, then we don't need greater resources. That represents a dangerous complacency about the competitive environment in which we exist. It is not a complacency anyone connected with the funding of external broadcasting can afford. It is like consistently under-investing in your product because you think the position you enjoy in the market today is satisfactory and it is therefore unnecessary to make further effort.

At 46 hours of Russian language broadcasting per week, we lag well behind our competitors in Radio Liberty (the US-financed Russian station in Munich) and the Voice of America. We need those hours to provide a range of output for the audience in the Soviet Union. It came as something of a surprise to us when we received an official suggestion that now that jamming was lifted we should reduce our Russian Service output, a suggestion that was hurriedly dropped.

Let me turn to the BBC's Polish Service, in some respects even more of a success story than our Russian Service. For them, jamming began in December 1981, just after the martial law emergency was imposed. All short-wave frequencies were blocked by interference. Naturally, when jamming was lifted from the Russian Service in 1987 we expected that the Poles would follow suit. The matter was raised informally and formally. Polish officials would cough, sometimes with embarrassment and regret, sometimes without. And, shrugging their shoulders in an easterly direction, they would imply that jamming was not a matter for which they were responsible. It was evidently one of the benefits of belonging to the socialist camp. However, we received unofficial signals that 1 January 1988 would be a very positive occasion, and on that day our short-wave signals entered Poland without obstruction, as our medium-wave signal had been doing throughout the years of short-wave jamming.

Here, too, the response of the Polish Section has been to reinvigorate their output. Fewer feature programmes are repeated; and a process of editorial renewal, similar to that being undertaken by the Russians, is also under way. The Polish Service staff have long been some of Bush House's most vigorous and determined journalists and they have turned their energies to a new pattern of current affairs programming. Their large and enthusiastic audience now totals 23 per cent of adult Polish listeners. Since 1980, despite the years of jamming, the audience for the Polish Service has doubled – a tremendous achievement in difficult circumstances.

This Service has been characterised throughout by a determination to talk to all sides of the Polish divide, to government and to Solidarity, and to non-Solidarity sources as well. This has not always been easy despite their best efforts. Yet they do pay off in the end. In 1987, when jamming was still in force, the Polish Government spokesman, Jerzy Urban, was invited to lunch at Bush House in an effort to improve the understanding between us. The exchanges over lunch were what diplomats describe as 'frank', yet, despite declining to be interviewed by the Polish Service when the lunch began, by the end of the meal Urban agreed to give the interview after all. During a recent riot at a Warsaw jail, a telephone call to Warsaw found a middle-rank government official at the other end of the line who quite openly gave the Polish Service his views on the situation. It is with such a genuine pursuit of openness that the Polish Service maintains its daily credentials of honesty, and readiness to paint the whole picture, to reflect as wide a range of opinions – including those within Poland – as it can obtain.

Having said that, it seems appropriate to set out the principles on which the BBC External Services have approached the difficult question of broadcasting to the Communist bloc, a question that was particularly challenging during the iciest days of the Cold War. I doubt if those writing in other parts of the BBC External Services would, or do, rely on different fundamentals, but the internal literature on broadcasting to the socialist camp is rather full, no doubt because it has been felt necessary to re-examine assumptions fairly frequently. It therefore provides a useful set of historical milestones to show us how we arrived at the present situation.

As long ago as 1971, a mere three years after the crushing of the Prague Spring of 1968, the then Head of the East European Service, Alexander Lieven, put pen to paper on the question of 'Broadcasting to Communist Audiences'. He warned of the ingrained scepticism of an audience which had learned from harsh experience that all sources of information were to be distrusted. They wanted accurate news of the outside world; they did not need to be told that Communism was discredited, their daily lives were evidence of that. So how should we approach listeners so professionally schooled in their scepticism? Lieven concluded:

> *All this imposes on us a particular need not only to be, but also to appear to be well informed, authoritative, balanced and fair in our output on Communist affairs. We should not adopt an automatically hostile attitude, avoid the 'black and white' approach and, at all costs abstain from pettiness, pinpricks, rubbing salt into the wounds, sarcasm, polemics or superior 'holier than thou' or 'you are always wrong' attitudes. A cool, detached, almost clinical approach is called for.*

It is a great sadness for those who worked with Alexander Lieven, and those, like myself, who met him late in his professional life as a friend, that he died suddenly in 1988.

In 1971, as Lieven summed up in his paper the consensus views of his department on their broadcasting philosophy, that greatest of BBC commentators on Soviet affairs, Anatol Goldberg, also set out his thoughts on his work. He told a graphic tale of how not to broadcast to the captive audience on the other side of Europe:

> *To ensure credibility, presentation is just as important as content. At the time of the 'Spring in Czechoslovakia' – when every word we broadcast to Russia about events in that country was dynamite from the Soviet point of view – a not very experienced colleague was about to introduce a talk on this subject with the remark: 'And now we are going to tell you about events which your press prefers to pass over in silence.' This kind of pinprick would have ruined the talk, since it would have been tantamount to saying that we were giving the information to Soviet listeners only because we knew that it would annoy their Government. Soviet listeners are very sensitive to this sort of thing.*

I should say that this cool, clinical, even dispassionate style had, and has, its critics both inside and outside the Soviet Union. The Russian novelist, Andrei Amalryk, complained when he visited the BBC that its output showed what he called 'a certain wishy-washiness: on the one hand . . . on the other . . . I suppose that is how the British are'. And no less a giant of Soviet dissidence than

Alexander Solzhenitsyn insisted on visiting Bush House to explain in magisterial terms that this very British approach to events in the Soviet Union was misguided and irrelevant. He indicated that he would be ready to provide his views on the correct way to broadcast to the Soviet Union. This he did in a 90-minute monologue, delivered from minutely written notes on small pieces of checked paper in several colours of ballpoint pen. The essence of it was that the approach of the Anatol Goldbergs of this world was no better than 'water trickling through your fingers'. On an earlier occasion he attacked the BBC Russian Service's attempts to improve their radio presentation by declaring memorably, 'Russia is not for dancing.' His conclusion delivered, the great man left. A month later the Director-General of the BBC, Charles Curran, received a letter from Solzhenitsyn. He explained that he had told the man Mansell, then Managing Director of the External Services, what was wrong with the Russian Service only a few weeks ago. Clearly he had done nothing; what was going on?

Solzhenitsyn was looking for a more engaged type of broadcasting, for the approach of a *journal de combat*. This is not an approach open to us even if we believed in it. The BBC broadcasts to the free, the not-so-free, and the utterly unfree. We broadcast in the same tone of voice to all of them or, as the former Controller, European Services, Peter Frankel, put it in 1984:

> It does seem to me essential for the reputation of the BBC – and for the personal integrity of its staff – to speak with the same voice of torture in Spain or Greece or Latin America as in the Soviet Union, while not losing sight of the scale of repression.

And this is exactly what we attempt to do. Such an approach is consistent with our principles, our objectives and our obligations. It is also, as the audience figures show, successful, for the reasons set out by Lieven and Goldberg in 1971 (the listeners can spot propaganda at 1500 metres). In 1986 a group of former Czechoslovak journalists wrote to us setting out their comments on foreign broadcasters. What was revealing was the hostility of their response to the Voice of America practice of broadcasting a daily commentary 'which expresses the view of the US government'.

This is a practice that the VOA continues to this day. The Czech former journalists commented:

> *When VOA first announced a commentary 'expressing the view of the US government', listeners in Czechoslovakia were flabbergasted. Why, oh why, has VOA taken to putting out outdated and naive propaganda? The first of these commentaries sounded just like Prague Radio in reverse, with their primitive and often shameless arguments. The programme reminded us of circulars and news-sheets put out by the party's propaganda department. 'When Radio Prague launches such a stupid propaganda tirade, I switch off. So why should I listen to something similar from VOA?' Alas, this is how a considerable majority of Czechoslovak listeners have reacted.*

Such views, and the number of letters and phone calls commenting favourably on our objectivity, reinforce my belief that the tone of voice established in the early 1970s is still effective today.

But that is not the end of the matter. The world of international communications is more complicated today than it was in 1971. It is far more diverse and far more susceptible to analysis. As research improves and the Soviet Union opens up, we also find out rather more about the way our audience listens. It is significant that an Institute of Public Opinion has been created in the Soviet Union under Tatiana Zaslavskaya whose devastating critique of the performance of the Soviet economy in 1983 is one of the founding texts of the present policy of reconstruction and acceleration.

After Chernobyl, Radio Liberty research in Munich carried out a brief survey of Soviet visitors to the West, to pull together clues about how Soviet listeners gathered their knowledge of that dreadful event. Thirty-eight per cent of the 214 respondents cited Western radio stations as their first source, compared with 31 per cent who heard of it first on Soviet television. Once they had heard the news on their own media, 53 per cent of the sample said they turned to Western radio for additional information. Selected comments from respondents were harsh: 'When Soviet TV started to broadcast about Chernobyl, we didn't believe what was said. Since they'd been silent it meant they were hiding something and if they were hiding something they must have been lying.' Or, more critically, this from a Lithuanian agricultural worker:

> *If the Western radio reports exaggerated a bit, it's the fault of the Soviet authorities who are used to hiding information of serious significance from the whole world. I think Western radios were right to warn the world about the accident's dangerous consequences.*

There was criticism from the other side too, some harsh comments from respondents identified as Party members: 'As is always the case in such circumstances, Western propaganda has tried to use the tragedy at Chernobyl to discredit the Soviet Union and its leadership.'

I am glad to be able to round off this section by telling you that in April 1988 the BBC World Service commissioned and broadcast a production of *Sarcophagus*, Vladimir Gubarev's starkly honest drama about Chernobyl. The production carried a dedication from the entire cast and production team to those who died in the attempt to lessen the impact of the potential catastrophe. I am proud of that gesture and the decision to broadcast that play.

So they listen because they need to know; they listen to us to check up on the official media; they listen to the official media to check up on us. Listeners in closed societies throughout the world have learned that grains of truth have to be gleaned diligently from what they see as clouds of chaff. We must never underestimate their seriousness, their wariness, their scepticism, their knowledge, their patriotism, or their intelligence.

But there may be a further reason for one part of the audience in the Soviet Union to listen to the BBC – and no doubt the VOA as well. The audience I have in mind are the senior Party leaders and cadres, the political intelligentsia (those that speak English and receive various digests of English broadcasts). It is at least conceivable that the reason they never permitted the BBC World Service to be jammed was because they wished to be kept informed about world events; they certainly realise that the Radio Moscow World Service gives a very limited world view. I was in Moscow some three years ago. Listening to the 8 o'clock Moscow bulletin I dozed quietly through a series of lead stories about demonstrations for peace and against nuclear weapons in cities throughout the world. I woke with a start to hear an unheadlined story well down the bulletin – the assassination the previous evening of the Swedish Prime Minister, Olaf Palme. Clearly, there was something very odd about Radio Moscow's news judgement.

With such values in the official media, the Soviet political and Party intelligentsia needed to keep themselves well abreast of events in the real world. How better than through the BBC World Service, to which (as anyone connected with it has often been told by senior Soviet officials) they regularly listen. On the night of the US bombing of Tripoli in 1986, I was preparing for a discussion in Moscow with the Brooklyn-accented Radio Moscow answer to Norman Mailer, roly-poly Joe Adamov. He was up-to-the-minute in his knowledge of the turbulent events of that day. Like a stooge feeding the lead comic his line, I said: 'How do you know all this?' 'Why from your World Service, of course.' One of my predecessors was sparring gently with a Soviet Ambassador at an international conference on the subject of information and disinformation. 'I suppose you would regard the BBC World Service as disinformation,' inquired Gerard Mansell. 'Of course,' replied the Russian with a straight face. 'I disinform myself every morning.'

But it goes even further than the need to remain informed about the world. Soviet Party intelligentsia may well regard the BBC and the VOA as absolutely essential indicators of the political mood in the West, at least as important as the conversations of diplomats. If there were a real darkening of the international scene, even a hardening of political attitudes as a result of some international crisis, they would, I believe, expect to detect it through our broadcasts – not through specific words but through the general tenor of those broadcasts. I am not saying that they would wait to pick up the specific government statement – they get those from the usual sources. More subtly, I think they would see the BBC World Service as a true sounding-board of Western opinion and thought, far broader than the opinions and policies of governments, more sensitively shaded and nuanced, more reliable because not motivated by the principal intention of influencing Soviet policies and actions. If that is true, and it is only a theory, the BBC (and the World Service in particular) is taken as a para-political hotline of communication about the West for the highest levels of policy-information in the Soviet Union.

Yet, useful as it may be to them and notwithstanding *glasnost*, there is no reason why the Soviet leaders should want their people to listen to our broadcasts. And the fact that they do is a constant reproach to the Soviet media. In March 1987 the following exchange occurred in Radio Moscow:

Voice 1: . . . A person who's heard a news item wants to know more about it the following day. And we must satisfy that wish of his quickly, and give a commentary on the event. Since people for a long time didn't receive full information about what was happening in our country and in the world . . .
Voice 2: . . . particularly in our country. People listened to the BBC mainly for news from Moscow . . .
Voice 1: . . . That's right, this phenomenon arose because of this.

In Poland the official counter to the previously forbidden fruit of listening to foreign broadcasts has been to play down the size of their audiences and to start a new programme wholly devoted to extracts from Western radio called *The West Speaks*. Whether Polish listeners will decide to rely on the state for its edited version of what we broadcast or whether they will stick to the habits developed over several decades will be proved in the years ahead. Experience suggests that dramatic changes will have to occur in the state broadcasting systems before their listeners willingly choose them as their prime or sole source of news, even – or indeed especially – about Western news broadcasts.

There is no doubt that the Soviet media have attempted to make their output more watchable, more credible, more relevant or more readable. Almost every traveller returning from the Soviet Union carries tales of how much *Pravda* has improved or how much more watchable is the main 9 o'clock news bulletin *Vremya*. And yet there is no reason for readers and viewers to give them the benefit of the doubt. They are still controlled by the Party as part of its propaganda policy. Certainly we do not assume that we have an automatic audience in the Soviet Union any more than we make that assumption anywhere in the world. But I was struck by a letter our Russian Service received in 1988 from a listener in Moscow who has tuned in for the last 20 years. He explained his previous reluctance to write. It was due to what he called the tradition of the Soviet post office, that is to say 'losing in transit 90 per cent of all correspondence addressed to non-Communist countries and about 75 per cent of correspondence coming from them'. What spurred him to write was the recent assertion by our former Moscow correspondent, Kevin Ruane, that Soviet listeners were switching away from Western broadcasts because of the impact of *glasnost*. I quote in full this correspondent's robust comments on that frequently made assertion:

People in our country really have of late begun to devote significantly more time and attention to the homeland's papers and magazines, to her radio and television, and there is nothing surprising in this: if in the past their pathologically mindless, bombastic lying evinced no more than contempt, and familiarisation with their content required 15 minutes a day at most, nowadays they have started to touch on really vital and important problems – and also in their lying they have begun to be cleverer.

But the consequences have turned out to be not quite those which the authors of perestroika *and the new thinking were counting on. Although strictly circumscribed, the access of oxygen has not only failed to stop the obvious decaying of the system: it has merely quickened the processes of its decomposition. The dethroning of erstwhile idols and former slogans has not brought forth new ideals: it has merely strengthened generalised cynicism. The absence of even the tiniest change for the better in the utterly squalid everyday sameness of life in the Soviet empire has merely intensified the scepticism and lack of faith in the possibility of any improvements whatsoever in the framework of the existing system.*

Unaccompanied as they are by any real deeds, the promises of Party leaders more than ever evince only irritation and ridicule. And thinking people can take no satisfaction from glasnost *released by order from above in homeopathic doses. They are less and less willing to accept on trust the claims of official agitprop that, despite all the regime's horrors, 'errors' and evildoing, despite poverty without issue and absence of rights, we have in our country the 'best of worlds'. And in search of truth, they turn to a trusted source, to the voices of the free world ringing in the airwaves, among whom one of the most important places belongs by right to the BBC.*

Now that is one letter only. And I don't attach undue importance to a single letter – even a letter written with such intelligence and perception and one that does pull you up rather short. We certainly must not be beguiled by it; we are not constructing a policy of it; but it does have the ring of commonsense psychological truth to it.

We shall continue to broadcast to the socialist bloc as we broadcast to other audiences throughout the world. We do not have one voice for friends and another for enemies. Both will enjoy news bulletins written in the same newsroom as the World Service, the French Service, the Hindi, Brazilian, Vietnamese, Cantonese or any of the 37 languages in which we broadcast. They will work to the same editorial standards as the other services in Bush House. And we will continue to deliver them all at an economical cost. We have 120 million regular listeners to our direct broadcasts. There are many millions more who listen to local relay of our broadcasts. At an all-up cost of £120 million in 1988 – capital and current – we deliver our message at a cost of 2 pence per listener per week, every week, every year. Not since the days of Rowland Hill and the Penny Post has Britain had such good value for money in any field of communication. No other medium can talk to a mass world audience so fast, so credibly, so effectively, or anywhere near so cheaply.

My aim is to deliver an even better editorial message more effectively and at least as cheaply as we have done in the past.

This chapter was first delivered as 'Broadcasting after Glasnost' to the European Atlantic Group on 20 April 1988.

THE WAY AHEAD FOR BROADCASTING TO WESTERN EUROPE

Although the BBC French and German Services first made their voices heard more than 50 years ago, I do not intend merely to praise them, and for that praise to be a decent prelude to burial. Rather, I submit that these two Services are adapting fast to the changing broadcasting environment of Europe and this process of adaptation provides a secure foundation for their continuation. I will also argue that the BBC World Service as a whole would be a weaker and less credible institution if its Western European wings were to be savagely clipped. But I will begin at the beginning, because the history of these two Services contains lessons that are still relevant today.

There was nothing calm and orderly about the birth of the French and German Language Services. Our established broadcasts in English had been joined a few months before by Arabic and by Spanish and Portuguese for Latin America – all in the context of Mussolini's expansionist policy in the Arab World and growing Nazi influence in Latin America. These Arabic and Latin American Services had been the fruit of lengthy debate and considerable advance planning.

Then, on 27 September 1938, the BBC was suddenly asked by Downing Street to stand by to broadcast the Prime Minister, Neville Chamberlain's, pre-Munich broadcast, in three languages: German, Italian and French. The broadcast was scheduled for 8 pm that same evening, and the Foreign Office promised to provide speakers and translations. At 6 pm, they called to say that they could produce neither speakers nor translations in French or German and the BBC would have to do the job. The result, according to a memoir of the period by Cecilia Gillie, a Senior Talks Assistant in the French Service, 'was chaos. No one in the BBC realised how long it took to make a translation of this kind. Finally a human chain was made from typing room to studio and sheets passed from hand to hand.' Who was to do the broadcast? According to Gillie:

> *Walter Goetz, who made the broadcast in German, told me how he was telephoned by J. B. Clark, then Acting Controller (Overseas), at a cocktail party and asked to come to the BBC on urgent business – ignoring the traffic lights if necessary. He drove at all speed to Broadcasting House and, a little stunned, as he had never broadcast before, and had in addition been drinking vodka, agreed to read the text, which was given to him page by page.*

It is small wonder that the official BBC report on that historic event observed that 'there had been inevitable delays and stumblings by the announcers, which caused unfavourable comment in many quarters and spoilt the effectiveness of Mr Chamberlain's speech. But in view of the difficulties under which the work was carried out this was excusable.'

The fact that this scrambled broadcast in chaotic circumstances marked the start of the French and German Language Services makes the event truly excusable. Daily broadcasts in French and German continued on an ad hoc basis for a month; then, in October 1938, the BBC and Foreign Office agreed to make them permanent. So they have remained to this day – and so, I shall argue later, they should remain for the foreseeable future. The story of the work of the French and German Services during the war is a relatively familiar one and I do not intend to repeat it in detail. They grew steadily from news bulletins alone, to bulletins and analytical talks, to lengthier transmissions, to a situation where their impact made them significant players in the wartime scene.

The French Service included those historic broadcasts by General de Gaulle, recalled by Cecilia Gillie as 'the ideal VIP broadcaster. He arrived on time, with a well-prepared script. I do not remember ever hearing him fluff. He was courteous and always found time to thank the recording engineer after he had finished.' It was Cecilia Gillie too, who created a vivid and effective programme format for the French. Jacques Duchesne, the *nom de micro* of the theatre director Michel Saint-Denis, led a trio of regular discussion panellists whose roles were as formally delineated as traditional characters in Commedia Dell'Arte. Duchesne provided the common sense and balance in talking about current events; a second broadcaster injected a somewhat Gallic combination of what Gerard Mansell, a former Managing Director and also the historian of the External Services, calls 'clear logic and a peremptory tone, softened by friendship'; the third played the fool, and usually a rather pessimistic one, often expressing the view that the war could not be won.

It was the French Service that carried the broadcast by the Prime Minister, Winston Churchill, live from the Whitehall War Room. Jacques Duchesne rendered the text into French – Churchill instructed him 'not to make it too correct' – and of course they demolished a bottle of brandy in the process. Harsh and gloomy as the situation was in October 1940, the closing words Churchill growled must have left many with the stubborn belief – irrational as they no doubt feared it to be – that all would yet be well:

> *So, good night, sleep well, gather your strength for the dawn, for the dawn will come. She will rise, shining for the brave, sweet for the faithful who have suffered, glorious on the tombs of the heroes. Long Live France! And long live also the rising of the brave of all nations who seek their lost patrimony and march toward a better time.*

At the end of the war Georges Bidault, President of the National Resistance Council, testified to the role of the BBC French Service in helping French listeners to withstand the lies of the Nazis and their Vichy collaborators:

> *Like a compass to the sailor, the wireless was to them the guide, and the assurance which at the height of the tempest, saved them from despair. It is partly, indeed largely, thanks to you, dear familiar voices, that our minds stayed free while our limbs were bound.*

The success of the Anglo-French team which made the broadcasts was a remarkable one. Darsie Gillie, the Head of the French Service, wrote of his French colleagues that 'their independence of judgement, their readiness to understand our difficulties and at the same time their firmness of principle in all important matters will remain as proof that co-operation between our two nations is both possible and very fruitful.' Twenty years later, Tangye Lean, Director of External Broadcasting, analysed the active ingredients of this intellectual cocktail as 'the intelligent understanding combative host and the brilliant European guest who worked together without hierarchical considerations to make bloody good programmes'.

In the case of the German Service during the Second World War, the situation was altogether more complicated. To start with, there was amazing concern and hesitation about the propriety of even broadcasting in German to Germans. Would there be reprisals with 'German listeners feeling we were propaganding'? In more positive mood, the Director-General received a proposal that, as a token of Britain's peaceful intentions towards Germany, the sound of the nightingale in Bagley Woods should be relayed across the continent. History does not relate, says Gerard Mansell, whether this preposterous idea was ever realised in practice.

Like the French Service, the German Service was responsible for memorable broadcasts. It was in a broadcast talk that Sefton Delmer rejected Hitler's so-called final appeal for peace before the government did: 'We hurl it right back at you, right in your evil-smelling teeth.' It was the Service which broadcast the programme *Hitler Answers Hitler*, where the latest claims from the Führer's tirades were contrasted with earlier, usually contradictory claims from previous utterances, and worked increasingly and devastatingly to his disadvantage.

It was the German Service which carried regular talks by Thomas Mann, urging Germans to bear the responsibility for creating Hitler and therefore their responsibility to overthrow him:

> the weapons for the enslavement of the world are the work of your hands and Hitler and his war cannot continue without your help. Stay your hand and help no more. For the future it will be of enormous importance whether you Germans yourselves put away this man of terror or whether it has to be done from outside.

If the two Services succeeded in engaging with an unprincipled enemy without ever being dragged down to the enemy's level, that was because the principles of wartime broadcasting had been securely defined from the beginning. There was, fortunately, a national consensus on this subject. Walter Monckton, Director-General of the Press and Censorship Bureau at the Ministry of Information, encouraged the BBC to follow its public-service instincts and tell the truth:

> *We simply must hammer home your main point – full and prompt news. Slowness conjures up a picture of reluctant extraction of teeth. Suppression in modern conditions fails, save in the few exceptional cases. But if we are prompt and candid our news service will be trusted and the reputation of the BBC will be enhanced for all purposes.*

And the *Evening Standard* supported the BBC's argument in March 1940, when official delays in announcing details of the German attack on Scapa Flow enabled the Nazis to win an international propaganda coup – albeit a brief one:

> *The old saying that a lie gets halfway round the world before truth has time to get its boots on could be hung in the offices of every government department. Delay and suppression encourage rumour. And rumour will run errands for Dr Goebbels but never work for us. Sealed lips are as dangerous as careless talk.*

The determination to be first with the bad news, to be frank about defeats, never to conceal knowingly, proved a sound basis – the only basis – for answering a propaganda war with actual truth. Then, as now, the maxim for World Service broadcasting holds good: we cannot expect listeners to believe that we tell the truth about the world outside if we conceal the truth about ourselves. As William Haley, the Director-General, summed it up after the war:

> *The British conception of news as something coldly impersonal and objective, having as its only touchstone accuracy, impartiality and truth, is one of our great services to a civilisation in which speed of communication gives news an overwhelming importance it never had before.*

Those observations, too, remain valid as a description of our broadcasting philosophy. If the need to be coldly accurate in an era of accelerating communications was paramount in 1950, it is certainly no less so in the still more intense and immediate media environment of today.

The French and German Services, then, had a good war; few better. Adjusting to peace, as for so many returning demobbed servicemen, was more difficult, though not so difficult for the broadcasters – they were working to principles that had not been put into khaki. But adjustment for the governmental policy-makers, the prescribers of External Broadcasting, has proved far more problematic. It remains true now, as in the post-war years, that Foreign Office policy-makers appear to value broadcasting to the enemy rather more than talking to friends. This difficulty in defining the value of dialogue with open societies, and setting it in a proper theoretical framework, is one that has caused frequent problems between the BBC and the Foreign Office. The debate has ebbed and flowed for some 40 years. It was therefore with some interest that I turned to the words of some of my predecessors as they undertook the same task I attempt today: charting the future role of these two great language services, as they stand on the edge of their maturity.

The first such attempt appeared under the signature of Sir Ian Jacob. As Director-General of the BBC, he introduced an official coming-of-age booklet in 1959, setting out the record of the European Services during their first 21 years. The 1959 booklet examined the way the entire European Service had made the transition from war to peace, albeit a peace in which broadcasting to a newly hostile Eastern bloc had become a major component. It was necessary to maintain a balance, the authors argued. 'It would have been intolerable for the European Service to concentrate on the Iron Curtain audiences alone and leave listeners in friendly countries without any opportunity of hearing British news and views through the familiar medium.' The importance of such balance is just as great today.

The authors of the booklet noted that despite the new circumstances in which broadcasting to Western Europe was taking place, an audience had still been retained; and they pointed to the importance of having a British broadcasting voice active in a European environment where the new European institutions were developing fast and where Britain was not part of them. They also saw rebroadcasting of our output on local radio stations in Germany as an established feature of the scene and they looked ahead confidently:

> *Under modern conditions it seems likely that contributions to the home broadcasting of other countries will become an increasingly important outlet whereby the European Service will reach large audiences in friendly countries. But it will long need to be linked with the continuance of direct broadcasting from London.*

Finally, the booklet noted that 'changed conditions may call for new techniques and new approaches to the problems of broadcasting in Europe'.

Perhaps most significantly, the 1959 coming-of-age booklet ended with a contribution from Sir Robert Bruce Lockhart, wartime head of the Political Warfare Executive (PWE). He could view the European Services as an outsider, and yet also as an insider because of the closeness of his wartime work with them. Bruce Lockhart made two important observations, both relevant today, more than 30 years later, though often ignored or undervalued. The first went as follows:

> *Broadcasting in the External Services cannot be turned on and off like a water tap. An important task of the European Services is to maintain in being services which may suddenly become important in the event of an unforeseen crisis. It is therefore unwise to close down one service on the advice of one or two persons because, once disbanded, the personnel are scattered and cannot be brought together in the not improbable event of a crisis. Broadcasting services have to be kept in a state of readiness, like battleships in former days and for the same reason.*

The simile may be a shade military for our tastes today but I applaud the sentiments unconditionally. And on the question of battleships, it is perhaps worth observing that the entire current and capital costs of the World Service for one year – totalling £110 million – actually amount to less than the cost of a single modern destroyer.

But Bruce Lockhart advanced a further argument in favour of maintaining Britain's voice to the free societies:

> *Bush House has played a significant part since the war in the renewal of ordered life in Western Europe and in the unity of Western civilisation. For London is a world news centre and there has been an arresting story to tell of Britain as a pioneer country, adapting historic institutions to a changing world. It is the cultivation of mutual understanding by the presentation of news and views which serves to link the countries of the Free World.*

The second survey of the rationale for broadcasting to Western Europe was made in a formal way by James Monahan, then Controller, European Services, in a BBC Lunchtime Lecture in October 1963. Monahan regretted the way in which Western European broadcasts had been more or less starved of resources since the war. He pointed to the increasing size of the radio audience in Europe and emphasised what he called the 'special advantage of sound radio over other means of information and persuasion from abroad – it passes through no intermediary. It does not require the favour of, for instance, a friendly newspaper editor; it goes to the listener direct.' He noted the 100 000 to 150 000 listeners in France, the 80 000 in West Berlin. Monahan chose not to compare the costs of broadcasting and its impact with alternative ways of spending such sums abroad. (Perhaps we are still too reserved on that score today.) But he was able to illustrate tellingly the truth of Bruce Lockhart's warning against stop–go policies in vernacular services. The Portuguese Service had been cut in 1957 but was restored in 1963, the year of Monahan's lecture. He observed drily:

> *The irony of it is that abolition took place – despite many protests – when Portugal was a safe friend of Britain and the restoration occurs only when and because there have been considerable rifts in that friendship. In fact, it must be taken not as a sign, however small, of a genuine reassessment of the BBC's potential role in Western Europe, but as a reminder that hostility not friendship is a qualification for receiving a vernacular broadcasting service from London.*

Reading it now, James Monahan may sound defensive – and no doubt he had reason to feel beleaguered. I do not intend to adopt such a tone and I believe that it is unnecessary to do so when looking to the future of the French and German Language Services.

Where does their future lie? First it is important to note their exact titles – they are the French *Language* and German *Language* Services respectively. This gives them a broader remit and a far wider responsibility than if they were narrowly targeted geographically. (It is BBC World Service policy to make the output of any service available where financially and technically possible to audiences outside their primary geographical areas.)

The French Language Service therefore broadcasts to Francophone Africa as well as to Metropolitan France. Of the 5½ hours a day that we broadcast in French, two-thirds goes to Africa, one-third to Europe. In Francophone Africa, the French Language Service faces competition from Radio France International (RFI), and from local international radio stations such as Afrique Number One from Radio Gabon. Afrique Number One is an international commercial station broadcasting 18 hours a day from Libreville in Gabon. And RFI broadcasts from the same 500-kilowatt transmitters. Voice of America is also an important competitor – 5 hours a day, Monday to Friday.

Nine international broadcasters broadcast more than we do, including the Soviet Union, China, South Africa and both Germanies. Nevertheless we come third in many places behind RFI and Afrique Number One. Overall figures are not available, but a survey in the winter of 1985–6 of the *urban élite in French-speaking Africa* by a Gallup subsidiary placed us fourth with 22 per cent.

In 1986 Deutsche Welle commissioned a comparative listening survey of themselves and the BBC's French output for Africa. It made criticisms of both, but it concluded that 'over a long period now the BBC has been moving forward, while Deutsche Welle has stood still'.

It is a good performance over a wide and competitive field. In Metropolitan France the audiences are of course small, though during the crisis of 1968 the listening swelled dramatically.

The two sides of the French Language Service reinforce one

another – the whole is greater than the sum of its parts. In particular, the credibility of the BBC's Francophone Africa operation depends on the maintenance of broadcasting to Metropolitan France. We are broadcasting in the world's second largest international language. The credibility of this output in Africa comes not only from its intrinsic quality but crucially from the knowledge that the broadcasts are destined for France as well. If programmes were made only for Africa, then they would be perceived as material intended only for Third World audiences and not for the Metropolitan French audience as well. Francophone listeners share that sense of Greater French cultural identity that is the particular gift of French colonialism. And a French Service for Africa alone would be diminished by not being part of that greater cultural unit.

The argument for the coherent unity of the entire German Language Service is analogous. An effective service must talk to both sides of the divided Germany and not only because it is economical to do so; credibility demands it. Both sides of Germany receive the same news, the same world coverage, and are addressed in the same editorial tone of voice. Were the programmes only aimed at the German Democratic Republic, then the audience reaction would be to see them as merely political in intention and therefore suspect or easy to dismiss as propaganda. Our broadcasts to the GDR draw, of course, on the pool of expertise and authority which supports our broadcasting to Communist Europe as a whole. But their effectiveness in the GDR depends in large measure on their also being made for the Federal Republic.

Starting from this fundamental philosophical position – that the services cannot be split – both the French Language Service and the German Language Service are taking active steps to broaden and diversify their audiences wherever they can. Both are now working to a coherent four-point strategy. I have mentioned the first part already – direct broadcasting to Metropolitan France (including Francophone Belgium and Switzerland) and Francophone Africa, in one instance, and to East and West Germany in the other (including Austria and German-speaking Switzerland).

The second element of the strategy consists of rebroadcasting. For the French this means gaining access to radio stations in the newly liberalised French radio scene. So far the results are encouraging. Rebroadcasters include stations in 78 French towns and cities, including Paris, Tours, Rennes, Blois and Quimper. In Belgium there have been legal barriers, but it seems these are about to come down, and we have already had a positive response from a national FM network. Oui FM, our rebroadcaster in Paris, recognised this in 1988 in a large ad in *Le Monde*. Drawing the attention of its listeners to the three BBC French news bulletins it now broadcasts each day, it described us as the best news service in the world. Coming from Paris, praise indeed!

Every time we gain another rebroadcaster, we not only tap in to a new audience but we win a free showcase for our products. If we had to buy the space, we could not possibly afford it. We get it free because they admire our programmes. In West Germany, the rebroadcasting takes a slightly different form – the sale and distribution of taped programmes to West German FM stations. This activity is showing encouraging growth. For example, the Service placed about 1200 items with German language stations in 1984; in 1987 this had risen to over 1900. Interestingly, the main growth area is in programme material dealing with Britain: we continue to be an object of great interest to our European neighbours. Our customers are not only the great public-service broadcasting organisations; in 1988 the new commercial radio stations started buying too – and in this case I do mean buying. We distribute through an agent in Germany.

The third ingredient in the strategy is to gain access to cable systems in the Federal Republic, and the German-speaking communities in Austria and Switzerland. While local regulations are exceedingly restrictive in all three countries, we intend to become a part of the local cable scene in all of them. The areas in which we are furthest advanced are Hamburg and Hanover, where we are already on these cities' cable network. We are also on a number of cable systems in Switzerland.

The fourth element in our strategy is of course BBC 648. This is the station identification given to the coherent presentation of our French, German and English output on the medium-wave frequency 648 which is audible in South-East England too. This frequency reaches with a good medium-wave signal into the golden triangle of the EEC. In the morning it includes a 1-hour block of

German, reinforced to provide more news and overnight despatches from BBC correspondents; a lively half-hour of French including a daily review of the British Press which we understand an extremely senior member of the Commission (Jacques Delors no less) uses to upstage visiting British guests on the contents of that day's London papers; and in English, of course, major planks of our World Service programming such as *Newshow*, *Newsdesk*, *24 Hours* and *The World Today*. We are providing a service of financial news together with travel and weather information. Capitalising on the fact that we broadcast from Europe's biggest financial centre we are introducing more frequent financial updates which will take account of overnight movements in markets around the world. And we are planning additional short news summaries in all languages to fit in better with the tight timetables of our business and professional audience.

We are pursuing the same approach with our 648 evening programmes: more interface between the French, English and German components of the schedule. In 1989 our transmission pattern was adjusted in order to incorporate into 648 our half-hour German news and current affairs programme *Heute Aktuell* which already goes out on other wavelengths at 5.30 pm continental time.

We regard this as a positive, significant and forward-looking four-part strategy to maximise the resources invested in both the French Language Service and German Language Service as a whole. And it was gratifying to discover a French government report on the future of external broadcasting – the Pericard Report prepared for Jacques Chirac – reaching similar conclusions to our own. Pericard lamented the fact that Radio France International is so far behind its rivals, such as ourselves; its output met neither France's 'ambitions or duties'; and its transmitter capability required massive reinvestment. In these two areas, government policy and investment in the first audibility programme have left the BBC World Service adequately placed, for the time being, in relation to our competitors. But the Pericard recommendations are a reminder of the intensity of competition that exists in the field of international short-wave broadcasting.

The Pericard Report then recommended that Radio France International should be the beneficiary of an ambitious development programme; and it advocated expansion of coverage in non-French languages. Most significant of all, it noted the importance of getting programmes on to local FM stations, and the importance of satellite delivery to provide the best possible coverage. It was encouraging to discover how many of our strategies have been identified as correct by our rivals and competitors.

But there is one further over-riding reason to believe that this policy is heading in the right direction – and that is 1992. If that date and the creation of a free internal European market yields what its advocates believe it will, then the position of the French Language Service and the German Language Service could be transformed. At present we are outside broadcasters in our target countries and victims of the heavy bureaucracy to which all outsiders are subject. After 1992, we shall be internal broadcasters with free access wherever there is a demand. It is our intention that by 1992 two services will have been established which are well placed to take advantage of such new opportunities. For what we have to offer is in short supply in the deregulated and often fractured media scene – a high-quality international news and information service which few new operators can possibly either afford or match.

But there are still further reasons for insisting on a stable future for these two services and they relate crucially to the standing of the BBC World Service as a whole. They involve three matters of principle.

Firstly, as I have said before, the overall tone of the BBC World Service depends on the fact that we broadcast to friendly countries as well as to unfriendly ones, to open societies as well as to closed ones. Were we merely to talk to the enemy, to societies with closed doors, the output would slide downhill to that dangerous point where it would be indistinguishable from propaganda or where it would certainly be perceived as such.

Further, it is important to talk to countries such as the United States and Australia because a demand exists for our output there. In some respects the US, though media-rich to a unique degree, is intellectually impoverished in the *quality* of its information as a result of the nature of its media. The country is not politically closed; but in view of its dangerous ignorance of Europe, its excessive concentration on the one or two flashpoints which the nightly news programmes designate as of US importance, its readiness to lurch from one extreme view of the world ('the USSR is the evil empire') to another ('Gorbachev is a great liberal reformer'), US opinion is in grave need of a broad and informed view of the complexities of the outside world. The BBC's role in talking to such open societies is different from, but surely just as important as, our role in talking to closed societies. But we talk to the latter more believably because we talk to the former too.

The second issue of principle is that we broadcast in foreign languages as well as in English. Vernacular broadcasts get far larger audiences than the English World Service in almost every country for which we have figures. It is a delusion to imagine that, great though the demand for English learning is, it will ever replace other languages as the medium in which large foreign audiences prefer to listen.

A recent survey of élite listeners in France and Germany – asking them to name radio-listening languages – showed 36 per cent of those questioned in Germany and only 22 per cent of those questioned in France naming English. This despite the fact that much higher percentages (96 per cent in Germany and 77 per cent in France) described English as a language they understood. It is because so many listeners – even well-educated ones – can only grasp a certain amount in English that we regard the trilingual 648 Service as so special and something which we in London are uniquely equipped to provide for the Europe of 1992 and beyond.

The third principle – an operational one – is that of continuity. The World Service has suffered too much from chopping and changing services in the past – but not mercifully since 1982. But politicians are always tempted to try and fine-tune broadcasting as if – as Bruce Lockhart complained – it can be switched on and off like a tap, even if a policy switch can be defined so precisely. Likewise, the Sinhala Service was cut in 1975, no doubt because Sri Lanka under President Jayawardene was deemed stable and friendly. Subsequent events make that decision a highly questionable one too. A decade ago, the BBC Burmese Service was listed for closure. Diplomats in Rangoon have assessed that 90 per cent of Burmese tune in and trust it. If in doubt, then, opt for continuity.

The experience of often small cuts in services has been, as Lord

Carrington conceded in 1983, 'wholly counter-productive'. None of us is much good at spotting the next crisis. As a former Director of External Broadcasting and subsequent Director-General of the BBC, Sir Ian Jacob, wrote in January 1957 on this very point:

To seek to save the cost of a particular language on the grounds that problems are unlikely to arise in that particular area is like an attempt to pick out the notes of a piano keyboard which will not be wanted . . . Broadcasting cannot contribute usefully to a solution of troubles magically after they have started. What is needed is time and stability of service to promote friendship on one hand and to eat into totalitarian situations by the steady action of truth on the other.

More than 30 years later, Jacob's remarks still hold good and have been vindicated by time and experience. The great languages of French and German represent major notes on the keyboard of international communications. It is imperative that we should continue to be able to play them.

This chapter was first delivered as '50 Years of Broadcasting to Europe – the Way Ahead' at the Royal Institute of International Affairs on 21 September 1988.

III

ISSUES OF PRINCIPLE AND POLICY

THE POLITICAL IMPACT
OF INTERNATIONAL
BROADCASTING

Speaking in May 1974, with a minority Wilson government in office, and the possibility of another minority government to come, Sir Michael Swann (then Chairman of the BBC) mused on the part that television had to play in this new era of political uncertainty. Did it create this public volatility? Or was television the crucible within which the ingredients of political consciousness – education, affluence, social mobility – were blended into a powerful destabilising brew? Sir Michael concluded with this observation:

> *Cynically one might sum it all up by saying that television simply confuses anyone who is not totally committed. Less cynically one might say that for the first time in history broadcasting gives every man the data on which to make up his own mind.*

That last sentence, applied to the field of international broadcasting, provides my starting point. Do the BBC External Services give people worldwide the data with which to make up their minds? Is this how we radiate influence? I shall take two cases in particular to assess how that influence demonstrates itself. And then I shall look at the arguments for and against our continuing to exert this influence in its present form.

Some background may be necessary, especially for those who have never heard the BBC External Services. Firstly, our UK audience is certainly an important part of our world audience and one that has every right to hear us since UK taxes pay for us. According to the BBC's five-year strategy the World Service is to be an element in our domestic network patterns, when the government's plans for frequency rearrangement go ahead as they have indicated in the Green Paper.

Outside these shores, we have broadcast for over 55 years to growing audiences. Each week we broadcast for some 750 hours in 37 different languages. Most people know about the BBC World Service, the 24 hour-a-day English language service which spans the world. But fewer people are aware of the strength of our vernacular services, ranging from the powerful Arabic Service (9 hours a day) and the Russian Service (6½ hours a day), to the more modest Tamil Service, or the Somali Service. Yet, of our total audience of 120 million regular listeners a week, a mere 25 million – if mere is the word – listen to us in English; while 100 million listen to us in their own language. To those of you with calculator minds, yes, you are right, five million listen in both English and their own tongue.

In some parts of the world, this foreign language broadcasting gives us a powerful reach into the local mass audience. In Nigeria, the Hausa Section commands 13 per cent of the adult population. In Somalia, all the evidence is that the capital and the towns fall silent when the Somali Service broadcasts from London. In Burma, the evidence is anecdotal only but it includes the personal testimony of a former Prime Minister of the country, U Nu, and tells us that listening is very widespread.

We have had encouraging news too from China. Until we opened a new relay station in Hong Kong directed to China, Korea and Japan, our signal to China anywhere north of Shanghai was weak to the point of inaudibility. Before 27 September 1987, the start of the relay, the Chinese Section received 900 letters a month, mainly from the south. In the first fortnight of the new relay they received 4000 letters – an eight-fold increase – mainly from the north and west, exactly the areas we had hoped to reach.

So why should all these people listen to international broadcasts? Surely, because their own news media are poor; because they are government-controlled; because they actively broadcast only propaganda. These people choose to listen to another point of view. Very often such listening is illegal, if not punishable. It is usually difficult: try finding a short-wave station on a cheap set with a remote signal at a time when you are not sure if there is anything there at all; or hunting for a familiar frequency when that frequency has been changed because the sunspot patterns have changed; or doing so through the fog of sustained and heavy jamming. Even to make the attempt represents an act of faith that leaves me awe-struck at the hunger for truth in a world where so much effort is dedicated to suppressing it. Yet hundreds of millions of people have made the effort, and made it successfully because of the revolution and capabilities of short-wave broadcasting. It defies barriers; it rejects restrictions; it bounds over mountains and seas; it is beyond accurate control; it often ends up in places where you would least expect to find it. It is the medium of freedom – and long may it remain so. In this medium, the BBC External Services have an honoured and successful place.

Yet it is too easy to bask in the pleasure of listeners' letters from unlikely parts of the world testifying to our reach and impact. It would also be misleading to suggest that there were no problems associated with it. There are, there always have been and there always will be. They occur when a perceived British foreign policy interest clashes with the needs and principles of British broadcasting. They did so in the latter days of the Shah of Iran when the Persian Service was accused by some of actually undermining the Shah and contributing materially to his downfall. Some believe it to this day. But what actually happened?

The BBC began broadcasting in the language of the country now known as Iran in 1940. During the war its performance won a wide audience for the BBC's accurate and impartial reporting. Yet from the very beginning its alleged influence was intimately bound up with the affairs of the country to which it was broadcasting.

In 1941, in the Persian Service's first year, it was held responsible by some for creating the climate of public opinion which led to the forced abdication of Reza Shah, father of the Shah. Certainly observers judged the influence of the Persian Service to have been powerful. Richard Dimbleby, then a war correspondent for the BBC, reported: 'I doubt if the power of broadcasting has ever been shown in such a way as by the success of these transmissions.' Another correspondent saw it as 'the first instance in history in which a ruler has been hurled from the throne by radio'. If so it was an extraordinary testimony to the power of a style of broadcasting which was little over a decade old. What mattered more was that the young Shah himself believed that the BBC was to blame for his father's downfall.

Yet if that experience lay lodged in one part of his mind, a later event should have shown him that broadcasting is always a two-edged weapon. In 1951 when the left-wing nationalist Prime Minister of Iran, Mossadeq, tried to nationalise British oil interests in Iran, the Shah and others must have been aware that the broadcasts from London – using the same tone as they had used when they had begun broadcasting a decade earlier – were at least a counterpart to the anti-British attacks of the Iranian media. It was not our purpose then or now to counter anti-British attacks; rather, our duty is always to report in such a way that listeners can judge events for themselves on the basis of facts, rather than distortion or calumny.

If the Shah did gain a more lenient picture of the Persian Service from the 1951 crisis, it was swept away in the far longer and more severe crisis that led to his own abdication in January 1979. In brief the Shah attempted a sweeping modernisation of his country using the vast oil revenues that altered the face of the modern world after the oil shock of 1974. His ideal was to westernise the country. He gave land to the peasants; he emancipated women; he set up large industrial enterprises; he bought Western arms heavily, and made no attempt to be anything other than pro-Western. In a mixture of scorn and envy, Radio Moscow disparaged the nascent Middle Eastern superpower and its leader as 'a sprat that has learned to whistle'. It was a revolution – what the Shah called a White Revolution – and it had little place for Islam. But the Shah had grossly underestimated the influence and power of the Islamic clergy and the hold they had on the nation. In particular he had underestimated the power of the Ayatollah Khomeini, with his hatred of Western materialism, and what he saw as the Europeanised posturings of the court gathered around the Shah.

The first complaints about the BBC were directed at programmes that were never broadcast on the External Services at all. A biography of the Shah by Margaret Laing was the subject of a Radio 4 interview in 1977. The Iranians lodged an official complaint against what they saw as 'extremely offensive . . . cheap, prejudiced, and inaccurate reporting'.

In the same year there was further protest about a BBC TV interview with President Carter. President Carter's enthusiastic espousal of the doctrine of human rights as a plank of US foreign policy was certainly one of the earliest blows to the Shah's position. But when pressed by David Dimbleby for a comment on the Shah, whose regime was accused of human rights violations, Carter refused to give it. The Iranians, however, protested that Dimbleby had insisted 'not once but three times in pressing for some condemnation of the Shah'.

Pressure on the External Services came from the Iranians themselves, through their Ambassador in London, or through the Foreign and Commonwealth Office, reflecting the urgent promptings of the British Embassy in Tehran. The British Embassy wanted the Persian Service closed down – there can be no doubt that it made their relations with the Shah and his entourage very difficult. For a time the prospect of closure was seriously contemplated. Yet cool heads and wise counsel prevailed. An official report concluded:

> the motives of listeners to the BBC in Persian are most likely the search for accurate, comprehensive and reliable news, including reports on events in or about Iran itself, whose centrally controlled national media provide a less credible vehicle. Or they may simply prefer the wider perspective offered by the BBC.

And it concluded that Britain gained goodwill and influence as a result of the broadcasts of the Persian Service as well as providing a vital counterweight to the broadcasts from other neighbouring countries including the Soviet Union. So powerful was the conclusion endorsing the Persian Service that when a hurricane destroyed the BBC Eastern Relay station in Masirah which projected a powerful medium-wave signal into Iran, the Foreign Office regarded its replacement as a high priority.

The volume of complaints grew as the political pressure on the Shah's government increased. In September 1978 the Persian Service was described, in a letter from the Iranian Ambassador to the Director-General, as 'a willing instrument for the *lèse-majesté* tracts of the Ayatollah Khomeini ... a tribune for his utterances ... were it not for the BBC and the wide audiences it commands, such exhortations to revolution would never have been disseminated in Iran'. The Service was accused of having instigated sabotage and arson, of broadcasting instructions on how to make petrol bombs, and of using a 'tone of abusive hostility and subtle menace'.

John D. Stempel, the official in the United States Embassy responsible for contact with the government in Tehran, actually said in his book, *Inside the Iranian Revolution*, that 'expatriate Iranians sympathetic to the revolution effectively "captured" the Persian Service of the BBC. While wrapping themselves in the flag of freedom of speech they proceeded to turn their broadcasts into an extension of the opposition's communications network.' The BBC's lawyers got the author to retract that totally baseless and defamatory allegation.

A self-professed Iranianist, J. D. Green, wrote in his work, *Revolution in Iran*, that the government's cut-down of news to its people drove information-hungry Iranians to the BBC: 'With characteristic ineptitude the government felt victimised by the BBC, yet itself provided no news so that people had no alternative to the BBC and other foreign news sources such as the VOA.' And he judges: 'If the opposition had been denied both its chief rallying-point, Khomeini, and one of its more crucial means of communication, the BBC, the revolution might never have gotten off the ground.' We can agree with the first 'if', while still disputing the unsubstantiated assertion that the BBC was Khomeini's 'crucial' means of communication. He had others of his own to rely on.

General Huyser, sent as President Carter's personal envoy to the military government, reported that the generals were obsessed with the BBC and its supposedly subversive impact. 'Cannot the United States silence the BBC's Farsi broadcasting?' he was asked by General Toufanian, a leading member of the Military Council effectively running Iran. Huyser concluded that 'the generals were about right about the damage these broadcasts were causing . . . I too was beginning to believe that the BBC news was probably slanted.'

The former Foreign Secretary, Lord George Brown, fired a broadside on Capital Radio in November 1978. He said the broadcasts had been 'tendentious, disruptive, partial and provocative' – the BBC had been acting as an *agent provocateur*. They had put the British business community and diplomats at very great risk and had helped to destabilise 'that vitally important country on behalf of an 80-year-old man, who was using the voice of the BBC to raise riots, violence and arson'.

The BBC's reply was crisp, delivered by Managing Director, Gerard Mansell the following week on Capital Radio: 'Utter rubbish.'

The leader of the opposition Conservative Party, Mrs Margaret Thatcher, visited Iran in the spring of 1978. Her office passed on to the BBC the complaints of Iranian ministers about what they saw as bias and inaccuracy in the Persian Service: 'It is hardly necessary to stress the political consequences which could follow if reports continue which are judged to be biased and inaccurate in their presentation.' Such a threat did the BBC pose in the eyes of the regime in Iran that somewhat desperate measures against the transmitters on Masirah and Cyprus were contemplated. Planning reportedly reached an advanced stage before the Shah reluctantly vetoed his enthusiastic followers' initiative.

This criticism was met with steady nerve by the External Services' management, who instituted a thorough check of every single item broadcast in the Persian Service in the months up to October 1978. Out of 460 such items, no more than six quoted Khomeini. So much for the persistent accusation that the BBC had let itself become a mouthpiece for the Ayatollah. Two Conservative MPs, the Chairman and Secretary of the Anglo-Iranian Parliamentary Group, went through the texts and agreed that there was nothing to substantiate allegations of anti-Shah bias in the output. In addition, a leading right-wing commentator unreservedly withdrew all allegations that some of the staff of the Persian Service were politically committed and had been recruited during the revolution. When it was shown just how well qualified the eight staff were and that none had been recruited during this period, the complainant, Brian Crozier, gave the service a '100 per cent clean bill'.

But that was not the end of the matter. A campaign of malicious rumour began against the Persian Service. Prominent British businessmen with connections and/or business dealings in Iran were handed what purported to be 'translations' of material broadcast on the Service. They were encouraged to complain to ministers in London. The material so distributed proved not to have been broadcast at all.

Senior staff at Bush House spent much time refuting familiar accusations. A closed-circuit relay of the Persian Service output was laid on to the Iranian Embassy in London. And the Persian Service broadcasts became some of the most monitored, checked and scrutinised journalistic productions in the history of international BBC broadcasting. They, and the staff responsible for them, emerged without blemish.

When confronted with this complete rebuttal of their specific charges, critics fell back on more general charges about the *manner* in which the staff of the Persian Service broadcast. They were accused of employing a sarcastic tone, of placing misleading emphasis, and so on. But actual recordings did not bear this out either.

At the end of November 1979 the Foreign Secretary (Dr David Owen) wrote to the Chairman of the BBC about the 'repeated complaints' from Iranian ministers and warned that the Iranians were on the point of expelling the BBC correspondent, Andrew Whitley. There could also be 'implications for British interests and subjects in Iran'. The letter called for the 'highest standard of objective reporting to be upheld' at this fraught time when so many in Iran were turning to the BBC for news. However, David Owen also reiterated the cardinal principle of non-interference in the BBC's editorial judgement.

The Chairman of the BBC, Sir Michael Swann, had a meeting with the Shah's Ambassador in London. The list of complaints was gone through yet again. And as usual they failed to bear out the charges of distortion, bias, and pro-Khomeini propaganda. One objection turned on the translation of a single word.

Yet for much of 1978 control of the press in Iran had been so relaxed that photos of the Ayatollah were appearing on the front pages of the newspapers in Iran. Their own media were telling Iranians far more than they could hear from the austere and meagre accounts on the BBC Persian Service. In view of this, the Chairman wondered why such a sustained and malicious campaign was being conducted against the Persian Service.

During this whole period the British government behaved impeccably. The Foreign Office maintained its 'hands-off' attitude throughout. It did its duty of relaying the complaints that were coming to it from many quarters. And it told the Shah and his ministers repeatedly that it had no editorial control over the BBC. The decision was entirely for the BBC and the BBC alone to make. The government would not interfere.

When the crisis was over and calm succeeded the storms generated by the revolution, when it was possible to view events in something like the clear light of common day, most of the BBC's critics admitted they had been misled or misjudged the situation. The British Ambassador in Tehran at the time, Sir Anthony Parsons, made a most handsome retraction. He compared the Iranian upheaval of 1978 with the year 1789 in France or 1917 in Russia. It was a time which had tried men's souls. It was inexplicable to those most closely involved how a strong, well-equipped army could be toppled by a motley of peasants, merchants, students and mullahs. But it was not right to blame the BBC. It was reporting perfectly fairly and, as he put it on BBC Radio 4 in 1984, 'telling the people of Iran in their language things that were actually happening in their country which the Iranian authorities were disguising from their own people'.

So, what was it all about? Clearly the broadcasts had an impact. Did they make a difference? Or rather, did they make the difference between the Shah's fall and his continuing in office? What the Shah's friends failed to recognise was that his fall was the result of his own actions – or one in particular. Until 1978 the Ayatollah Khomeini was in the holy city of Najaf in Iraq preaching opposition to the Shah in a way that the world at large was ignorant of. But in October 1978, as a result of pressure from the Shah, the Iraqi government expelled Khomeini to Paris, to the obscure suburb of Neauphle-le-Château, to which the world's media then beat a path.

However, there was one organisation that might be held at least partially responsible for the Shah's downfall. It was not the BBC but Philips, the manufacturers of audio cassettes. For Khomeini's sermons had their effect within Iran not principally from broadcasts but from the circulation within mosque and bazaar of cassettes carrying his denunciations of the Shah. There are times when even radio is not the most potent of weapons. But it is audible; it gets under the skin; it is always easier to blame the thing over which you have no influence than the things over which you do.

It is worth noting too that the same Persian Service that is alleged to have overthrown the Shah – presumably in the service of the Ayatollahs – was subjected to similar attacks from the Khomeini government. A couple of years ago I met an Iranian broadcasting official at an international conference. He was pleasantly berating the Voice of America delegate for VOA's alleged lies and distortions. 'We listen to you very closely,' said the official, 'and we have a pile so high of documents of your inaccuracies.' He gestured to indicate a pile three feet high. I did not wish to be spared such condemnation so I asked him if they monitored the BBC closely. The Iranian assured me that they did. 'Well then how big is the pile of our alleged distortions and inaccuracies?' He gestured to indicate a pile a mere twelve inches high. I registered disappointment. 'Ah, you British,' he explained, 'you are so tricky.'

Another incident where one of our vernacular services was allegedly involved in at least hastening a regime's fall was the collapse of the Thieu regime in Saigon.

By the end of the Vietnam War the influence of the BBC Vietnamese Service was deep and extensive. In 1974 a survey showed that four times as many people listened to the BBC as listened to the Voice of America. On 15 July 1975, the *Observer* correspondent, Mark Frankland (an old Vietnam hand), wrote:

> *In moments of crisis one sometimes has the impression that everyone with a short-wave radio does listen to the BBC – South Vietnam under the old regime was a case in point. As a British journalist one could go into some remote village and explain more or less who one was by uttering the magic sound BBC. Almost always there were nods of recognition and very often, too, a smile.*

Earlier, during the traumatic events of spring 1975, Martin Woollacott, a *Guardian* correspondent in South Vietnam, wrote on 23 March of 'the God-like authority of the BBC ... difficult to comprehend for those who have never visited Vietnam'. During the same period one of the South Vietnamese government's leading information officials told a visitor from the Vietnamese Section: 'Everybody here listens to you, of course.'

Given that such credence was attached to the Vietnamese Service, it was inevitable that people would in times of crisis act on the basis of the information supplied. By April 1975 the editors of the six leading Saigon newspapers wrote to the Director-General of the BBC alleging that the BBC 'has often released premature information which may be used as an indirect source, for the Communists, of intelligence about troop movements . . . Many innocent people have been killed in the present Communist shellings due to leaks . . .' There was never any indication of what specific information had been released. The editors said that the BBC 'often releases commentaries and distorted information which may hurt badly the fighting spirit of a nation which is fighting fiercely against Communist aggression'. And they instanced the reports broadcast by the Vietnamese Service of the withdrawal of the Army of South Vietnam from the Central Highlands along Highway 7B. This proved to be the beginning of the end for South Vietnam.

For five days the government had said nothing; the people learnt about the evacuation from London. An angry Thieu had forced the six editors to complain to the BBC. In his reply, the Director-General pointed out that many of these reports came from a Vietnamese correspondent of *Chinh Luan* (edited by one of the complainants) who had been quoted directly.

To provide the necessary background information, there are two towns in South Vietnam: one called Darlac, and another town to the south of Darlac called Dalat. The BBC announced the capture by the Viet-cong, on 19 March 1975, of Darlac. There was a mass evacuation from the area all around Dalat and it was widely rumoured that the BBC had said it was Dalat that had been captured. But our announcers in London, well aware of the danger of confusion, had taken particular care to pronounce the name clearly. The recordings proved it. We came to the conclusion that the refugees needed an excuse for their flight. The BBC as the most-listened-to station seemed to be the obvious scapegoat. To give another example, *New York Times* correspondent, Malcolm Browne, told a BBC visitor of refugees from Hue who had left their homes because the US Airborne had pulled out of Quang Tri – a fact they didn't believe until they heard it from the BBC.

All of this is certainly a tribute to the credibility of the BBC Vietnamese Service which throughout a long war had created and kept up its reputation for truthfulness in good times and in bad.

By the end of the war, the times were, of course, bad. But should the BBC not have reported the news that the US Airborne was withdrawing from Quang Tri? In fact refugees left because of the withdrawal, not because of the report. Does anyone seriously suggest that the reason for the collapse of the South Vietnamese military front was because we broadcast the news rather than because the North Vietnamese were in command militarily? At the time of the fall of Saigon, I was presenting the daily World Service programme *24 Hours* which went out at 13.09 GMT. I recall that a regular feature of the last weeks of the Vietnam War was the live contributions from Saigon by the BBC's South-East Asia correspondent, Derek Wilson. He would arrive in the studio each night fresh from the battle front – it was shrinking before his and other correspondents' eyes. He would then describe the experience of military collapse but of course only some hours after it had happened. I emphasise this point to show that the idea that the report can cause the event is logically and practically ludicrous.

But there is a further point. Should the BBC cease reporting once its reports start to have an impact on events? Neither we nor any other news organisation could possibly accept that as a basis for keeping faith with an audience who expect truth and accuracy under all circumstances. Reporting is not a fair weather activity; it is a duty for all seasons.

None of this would of course convince those at the receiving end. In his farewell address to the nation in April 1975, President Thieu accused the Vietnamese Service of causing the collapse of his government and so contributing to South Vietnam's takeover by the Viet-cong. Was he wrong? I believe he was – just as the Viet-cong were wrong in their response.

In July 1975 Derek Wilson was thanked by the Chairman of the Viet-cong, Nguyen Huu Tho. In a letter written on 30 July 1975, Derek Wilson quoted the Viet-cong Chairman as saying that the BBC had 'done much to help the revolution during those past few months'.

This attitude reflects a fundamental confusion in the minds of the audience – particularly the politically committed – which was thrown into sharp relief in the civil war in Uganda, where our broadcasts appeared to achieve a marked effect. In 1986 a member of the African Service's staff visiting Uganda was hailed by

President Museveni as 'a great freedom fighter who helped to get rid of Obote and that fellow Tito Okello'. The President spoke of the way in which the African Service had 'relentlessly exposed the tyranny in Uganda'. To loud cheers he concluded: 'I don't know yet how much aid we can expect from the British, but surely having helped us to defeat the dictatorships that have been killing our people, the British are not going to let us down now.'

Of course Museveni's last sentence confuses the BBC with the British government, but his real point was that since a British institution (the BBC) had helped in drawing attention to the violation of human rights in Uganda, then surely the British government should feel an obligation to 'follow through' with help to rebuild the country. The remark of a Ugandan lawyer (made to the same African Service visitor) was fairly typical of the feelings of a large number of Ugandans. He said: 'I couldn't understand why the British government had to leave it to the Americans to condemn the massacres that were going on here. But at least the BBC stood up to the butchers!'

In January 1986 Yoweri Museveni took power after five years of guerrilla warfare against the governments of Obote and Okello. In the two years before Museveni took over it was reckoned (by Amnesty International) that some 250 000 people, mostly civilians, had been massacred by government forces. The state-controlled radio and television services sought to conceal the extent of this blood-letting, whereas the BBC's African Service daily bulletins and programmes of analysis were a source of irritation to the regimes in power. The BBC stringer in Kampala was seen as a kind of folk hero. For President Museveni and many Ugandans the BBC therefore became a voice of truth and sanity in a mad, cruel and misinformed darkness. They perceived us as taking their side against the forces of thuggery.

The BBC does not, of course, 'take sides' in this sense. We are not 'neutral between good and evil' as some of our critics would have it, but we do not 'pick' a position and advocate it in the manner of a prosecuting barrister. Rather, we set out in any situation to tell those in the midst of the often appalling trauma (Uganda, Beirut, Sri Lanka, Afghanistan) just what *is* going on AS BEST WE CAN. We have to rely on human beings to find out and report the facts. It is these 'front-line' journalists who take the most tremendous risks, and who sometimes suffer injury and death in the course of duty, to whom we look for the raw material of our broadcasting. In 1987 our correspondent in Nairobi suffered a fractured spine when a member of the Kenyan police broke a club across her back.

The three cases I have mentioned – BBC broadcasts to Iran, Vietnam and Uganda – as different as they were in their historical development, had certain features in common. In all these situations, the BBC was broadcasting in the main language of those countries to a substantial mass of people in all sections of the community. This audience was largely in the dark as to what was happening in their own land because the domestic media were under tight state control. The audience was as large as it was because these domestic outlets did not trust their own people with information, but instead put out a stream of lies, half-truths, 'encouragement' and propaganda. In doing so they built up such a spirit of scepticism in their listeners and viewers that even when these domestic journalists came out with the truth they were not believed.

Again, in all these cases, the regimes in question, when looking for a scapegoat, lighted on the BBC. The Shah charged the BBC with losing him his throne; President Thieu accused the BBC of undermining the government of South Vietnam. In a reverse example, President Museveni saw the BBC African Service staff as fellow 'freedom fighters' who had helped overthrow Obote and Okello. It is flattering in a way to be credited with so much power, but a total misconception of our role. It was reality which dissolved these governments – the BBC was merely the harbinger of the facts.

Where does this leave us? I conclude that in international broadcasting, you have to take the rough with the smooth. Indeed, it is only the rough which makes the smooth credible. You cannot argue that the BBC must provide an accurate, impartial and unbiased news service and then qualify that by limiting coverage to events where Britain has no direct interest or, worse still, stop it altogether in places where Britain wishes to protect a particular interest, however important. For Britain has two types of interest – the immediate diplomatic one which demands a certain view and a certain policy; and the longer-term broadcasting one which demands that British broadcasts are always believed because over a wide range of situations they are found, through experience, to be true.

In cases such as Iran or Vietnam there was an apparent clash between the diplomatic and broadcasting interests. Yet we can see now – and many saw at the time – that to have gagged the BBC during either of these periods would have saved neither Thieu nor the Shah, but would have fatally wounded the External Services. It is gratifying that politicians across all parties accept this principle, but that is not to say that I would expect them not to complain if another Iran or Vietnam were to arise, as it will. I would also expect that we would behave with as much principle as we did then.

This chapter was first delivered as 'Radiating Influence – the Political Impact of International Broadcasting' at the University of Newcastle (Earl Grey Memorial Lecture) on 26 November 1987.

BETWEEN ACADEME AND FOREIGN POLICY – THE BBC'S BALANCING ACT

Between academe and foreign policy' – few titles could more aptly express the physical and psychological location of the BBC External Services. There they stand, at the end of Kingsway, that most dreary bit of town planning; the two somewhat improbable giants, holding aloft the torch of the unity of the English-speaking peoples, displaying a lofty confidence about their role and purpose. They represent, so I am told, Britain and North America. In fact, if we could look closer, I think we would detect not so much an assured upward contemplation of the ever-blazing torch, but a shifty sideways glance from each of them. Britain – if that is the figure on the right – is eyeing the London School of Economics (LSE) slightly to his right; his companion, North America, appears to be casting his thoughts to the Foreign and Commonwealth Office down in Whitehall to his left. They are not alone in doing so. The twin polarities of academe and government exercise their respective attractions very explicitly over Bush House.

Usually, when in balance, they allow us to maintain a proper equilibrium, though sometimes one sphere attempts to draw us more fully into its field. It is not the LSE alone, but King's College, the School of Oriental and African Studies, the major research institutes such as Chatham House and the International Institute of Strategic Studies (IISS) – these constitute the immediate intellectual reservoir from which the External Services have drawn much of their knowledge and many of their attitudes. For every trainee producer, the experience of meeting, talking to and learning from academics is extremely valuable. I certainly counted myself privileged during my training to rub shoulders with the late Professor Fred Northedge, Professor Geoffrey Goodwin, and many others.

Fred, who always maintained that the discipline of writing 4½-minute commentaries did wonders for his academic prose and teaching style, took part in the first editions of almost all the new current affairs programmes at Bush House over two decades and in many of the normal editions in between. What Polish crisis would be complete without Anthony Polonsky? What Eastern European developments without the staccato urgency of Geoffrey Stern or the Hapsburg cynicism of George Schopflin? What Japanese interpretation without Wolf Mendl from King's? What Middle East crisis unenlightened by the subtlety of Takis Vatikiotis? What slight shift in the international strategic defence debate was not clarified and put into perspective by the late Colonel Jonathan Alford from the IISS? And what a truly irreplaceable loss to us all his early death was. All these were, and continue to be, a vital part of my own education and of the current affairs community at Bush House.

So close is the connection that it occasionally gets taken for granted. In an article about the External Services in the *Guardian*, Alan Rusbridger asked: 'Okay, you make allowances for shoestring budgets. But is it really necessary every time there is an item on Ruritania to wheel on the same Reader in Ruritanian studies to pontificate?' Well, I didn't know there were two. While I have always discouraged the creation and maintenance of what used to be called in Bill Hardcastle's days 'The World at One Stage Army' or its Bush House equivalent, I do consider it proper that when events erupt in Utopia, Ruritania or Amnesia that we should be able to deliver a Reader in Amnesian Studies to comment. I would prefer not to have him or her the whole time but needs must where the devil and events drive. You will see that I make no apology for the close links between us and academe, and of course these are nationwide links and not merely confined to the immediate Central London campus which I have been highlighting.

And this flow of knowledge to Bush House also comes from further afield. The prime ministers and ministers from overseas who make themselves available to our broadcasters when they visit London are too numerous to mention. Increasingly, we find that we can persuade world leaders to expose themselves to the vagaries of the international phone-in. British Foreign Office ministers speak regularly either to the World Service or to one of the language services depending on their travel schedules. And debates between British MPs on key areas of international controversy have always been a feature of our broadcasts.

I remember in the 1960s the combative entertainment of the Rhodesian independence roadshow where Denis Healey and Patrick Wall became a familiar and much-loved twosome in the studios thrashing out the painful dilemmas of that issue. Or there was Peter Shore, fleck-lipped with emotion in his opposition to the EEC entry question; and the nerve-jangling clashes over Harold Wilson's peace-making efforts in Vietnam, discussing whether to back or condemn US policy in Indo-China. I hope and believe that the great issues of today are engaged fully by the External Services and that on the occasions when academics and policy-makers meet in our studios they make their own contribution to the exchanges. So in the contributors that we employ, the ideas we reflect, the controversies we explore, we sit easily between academe and foreign policy. It is a proper and comfortable ground to occupy. But let us go back to fundamentals and to the precise terms of reference under which we operate. The documents in question are the BBC Charter, the Licence and Agreement, and the Statement of Objectives of the External Services.

Clause 13.1 of the Licence and Agreement states that the BBC will send programmes efficiently 'from such stations as, after consultation with the Corporation, the Secretary of State may from time to time . . . in writing prescribe'. That is to say, the government can determine where our relay stations shall be sited.

Clause 13.5 states that the External Services will broadcast 'to such countries, in such languages and at such times as, after consultation with the Corporation, may from time to time be prescribed'. In theory and in practice, the Foreign and Commonwealth Office (FCO) has the power of veto over the opening of any new services; in practice the closure of existing services usually leads to a more equal battle, which the External Services, from time to time, win.

Clause 13.5 continues by saying that: *the External Services shall obtain and accept (from the Foreign Office) such information regarding conditions in, and the policies of Her Majesty's Government aforesaid towards, the countries prescribed and other countries as will enable the Corporation to plan and prepare its programmes in the External Services in the national interest.*

This refers to the practice of delivering Ambassadorial telegrams to Bush House which a few senior members then see. And this process is surrounded by a good deal of mystique; as if the exposure to diplomatic thinking would in itself shape the editorial line of those who read the messages. Let me demythologise them. If you were to take the contents of an average telegram, particularly a 'First thoughts' by an ambassador or a valedictory at the end of a posting, set it up in print and ask people in a blind test if they could tell the difference between that and a journalist's 'First thoughts' and a valedictory, I'm not sure you would notice the difference. To a far greater extent than is sometimes admitted, journalists and diplomats fish in the same pond for information. Their methods of getting information, evaluating it and verifying it are identical, so the resulting written material is unlikely to be wildly different.

Ambassadorial telegrams are not intelligence reports. Their contents may be passed in direct form for us to read for ourselves but they are in substance also passed on to diplomatic correspondents through Foreign Office News Department briefings, and they no doubt form the basis of private exchanges between diplomats and academics who are trusted and have an entrée into those circles. In short, to read a telegram is not to see the world with new eyes. For some I have no doubt that reading their first telegram is an anti-climax, like other great initiations in life. I am happy to say that mine was not. The late, great Ambassador in Vientiane, John Lloyd, was a true friend of journalists in the 1970s and showed me – and others no doubt – a detailed and highly informative cable on the state of the Laotian peace negotiations which was first-class copy in anyone's terms. There aren't many like that.

Let me add to this list of definitions of our obligations to government the first clause of the Statement of Objectives:

To provide an external broadcasting service to target audiences overseas in as many languages as are prescribed by the FCO as

*part of the pattern of priorities arrived at in consultation with
the prescribing departments and to plan and prepare such
broadcasts in the national interest.*

There is of course a final, practical point – money. The External
Services are directly funded by the government as part of the Foreign Office Vote. They – to use the obvious analogy – pay the
piper. Do they therefore call the tune? By no means.

The rubrics quoted here incorporate the sum total of our obligations to the government of the day. They are considerable. If
they were the only texts to which we could refer and under whose
terms we could operate, then I think it would be hard, in theory or
in practice, for us to be anything other than just another state-
controlled broadcaster, with as much – or as little – credibility as
they usually enjoy. Yet no one – except our worst ideological
opponents – would say that that is what we are or what we have
been for as many years as most of us can remember. This is in
large part because members of the External Services have interpreted their role with a robust independence.

Over 50 years ago the Arabic Service began its broadcasts, the
first of the 36 overseas languages in which we now broadcast. The
very first news bulletin carried a report of the execution by the
British authorities of a Palestinian Arab convicted of carrying a
gun. It was – you may think – a suitably independent way to start.
Rex Leeper, Head of the Foreign Office News Department, wrote
indignantly: 'Straight news must not be interpreted as including
news which can do us harm with the people we are addressing.'
Fortunately, however, the Arabic Service was already operating
under the terms of a classic definition by J. B. Clark, then Director
of the Empire Service, and later, as Sir Beresford Clark, to be Director, External Broadcasting:

> *The omission of unwelcome facts of news and the consequent
> suppression of truth runs counter to the Corporation's policy
> laid down by appropriate authority. If external bodies wish the
> Corporation to modify an established policy, under which I
> have been directed to guide its news services, suitable
> representations should be made in an appropriate manner.*

As a riposte to attempted interference with the integrity of the news operation it is perhaps a touch pompous by today's standards but I do not think its sense could be bettered.

That was not the end of the story, however. There was an instance – and a particularly lurid one – of the government attempting to influence the tone and content of external broadcasting, albeit in the emergency conditions of wartime. In March 1942, the Special Issue Sub-Committee of the Overseas Planning Committee of the Ministry of Information sent the BBC Eastern Service a note on how to deal with Gandhi in their talks. One of the talks writers was Eric Blair, otherwise known as George Orwell. After a detailed description of the proper tactics to employ, the paper concluded:

> *The limelight should throughout be focused (still bearing in mind the need for discretion) on the figure of Mr Gandhi, the inconsistencies of whose policy should be exposed, and who should be gradually built up as a backward-looking pacifist and Pétainist (in this connection his associations with prominent Indian industrialists such as Mr Birla could usefully be built up) who had become a dangerous obstacle to the defence of India and whose policies in fact, if not in design, play straight into Japanese hands.*

You could not ask for an attempt at clearer guidance than that.

Yet there was at least one even more highly coloured instance of attempted guidance, which threw light on the extent of the wartime determination to exert editorial influence. More worryingly still, it showed, in the words of W. J. West, editor of *Orwell's War Commentaries*, how 'thoroughly steeped in Communist Party propaganda some of the officials of the Ministry of Information were'. A lengthy Special Issue note outlined ways in which broadcasts should allay the ideological fear of 'Bolshevism', a fear spread, it was said, by Nazi propaganda. One section – typical of the whole – went like this:

> *If Stalin maintains the Comintern in being, it is merely as a second line of defence which will be proved superfluous to the extent that he can rely on the co-operation of Britain and the USA. We should note evidence to show that parallel with this development in Soviet policy there has been a change in the*

type of personnel in power in the USSR. The ideologues and doctrinaire international revolutionary types have been increasingly replaced by people of the managerial and technical type, both militarily and civil, who are interested in getting practical results.

Does that phrase have a familiar, contemporary ring? Thank goodness we resisted such guidance.

Such communications are unthinkable today. There are no remote equivalents of the Ministry of Information guidance notes – certainly not the telegrams. The Head of News Department would not contemplate any communication such as Rex Leeper's. If written, then its reception would be frosty. In fact the position has changed so much that in the *Guardian* article already referred to, Timothy Eggar, the Under-Secretary of State at the FCO, made this categorical declaration: 'There is no attempt to control the final output. One can only say look at the track record. If the thesis of FCO influence was a valid one, how come the World Service has got the reputation it has got?'

The answer to that question is of course that the External Services have to meet a set of obligations set out in our governing documents which define the balance between our responsibility to government and our responsibility as independent journalists.

The first constitutional anchor that maintains our position between academe and government is the BBC Charter. It demands that the BBC should be both independent and impartial, and makes the Governors responsible for maintaining independence and observing impartiality. World Service therefore exists firmly within a body whose Charter guarantees its independence and places on it an obligation to be, and act, independently. Such a sheet anchor is vital when the funding for World Service comes directly from a government body. There is tension between the two but the Charter obligations are immovable.

Thirdly, the World Service's Statement of Objectives defines the precise nature of broadcasting in the national interest. Primarily, it is to 'make programmes that are of a high professional standard, relevance and interest; to attract and retain audiences, and thus to enhance Britain's standing abroad'. The Objectives further define this general activity by stating an obligation to include 'a credible, unbiased, accurate, balanced and independent service of news covering international and national developments'. The significance of these Objectives – ratified by the BBC Board of Governors – is that they put journalistic and broadcasting priorities at the heart of the objective of broadcasting 'in the national interest'. Experience has shown that this set of values is the only secure way of being credible and effective and thus in any way providing value for money.

One set of demands and obligations – those which set out the government's policy priorities – tend to pull us towards one pole of attraction. The other set which I have just outlined – those which establish our professional values and intellectual obligations – draw us safely back into the equilibrium of independence.

Yet that reassuring conclusion depends on the government of the day accepting that the approach and criteria of the External Services will often be different from theirs. There will always be clashes between the immediate political needs of the government and the longer-term needs of the External Services, to which we have to adhere if we are to continue to be effective. Let us look at some of those clashes over specific policies and over the question of how the External Services should be developed in the national interest.

As we saw in the previous essay, the classic clash occurred during the dying months of the Shah's rule in Iran. There is no doubt that the Shah was deeply annoyed by the reports that the BBC Persian Service brought into his country of the growth of opposition and the swelling support for the exiled Ayatollah Khomeini; there is also no doubt that those broadcasts – and others – provided information which the government attempted to keep from its own people. The Shah certainly convinced himself that the Persian Service broadcasts were the primary cause of his deteriorating position and he told everybody – from American Envoys to British Ambassadors – that the BBC Persian Service was doing the damage and had to be closed down. The British Ambassador Sir Anthony Parsons put his weight behind these calls. However, the Foreign Office concluded after an inquiry into the work of the Persian Service that Britain gained goodwill and influence from their broadcasts, as well as providing a vital counterweight to broadcasts from other neighbouring countries including the Soviet Union.

Others too – including Sir Anthony Parsons himself – later concluded that while the provision of free information otherwise denied to the public was a potent factor, yet far broader factors were finally responsible for the Shah's fall. Perhaps the most important of these was the Shah's own mistake in pushing Khomeini from international obscurity in Iraqi exile to international media stardom in the Parisian suburb of Neauphle-le-Château.

Immediate British policy needs demanded, some argued, that what the External Services did for the Greeks under the Colonels, or for Uganda under Amin, it should not do when British interests appeared to be threatened. Longer-term views demanded that the consistency of purpose and treatment demanded to maintain External Services credibility *should* provide for Iran what we had provided for Greece or Uganda. Predictably, the Persian Service is regarded by the present Iranian regime with a hostility similar to that of the Shah. It is over such longer periods of time that an approach to international broadcasting is validated. Such consistency of analysis, undistorted by the short-term demands of policy, places us far closer to the values of academe than of Whitehall.

These instances occur all the time. In December 1987, the government of Bangladesh complained about the BBC's reporting of the opposition strikes and the attempts to overthrow President Ershad. Their complaints were essentially that the reporting was inaccurate, though they gave no details; that it was maliciously intended and calculated to undermine a government fighting for national unity; that the reports reflected the personal opinions of the staff of the Bengali Section of the BBC who – it was inaccurately alleged – were from, or sympathetic to, neighbouring and Marxist-governed Indian West Bengal. Not content with these charges, the government detained without trial Ataus Samad, the BBC local correspondent in Dhaka. After protests from us and Samad's other employers, he was released, having spent some 14 days in detention. The Bangladesh government then expelled the BBC correspondent, Phil Jones, and forbade citizens to communicate news of any kind to the BBC. I note only in passing that during and after the war that led to the creation of Bangladesh, the reporting of the BBC's Bengali Service was held in the highest esteem in those very governmental circles that later reviled it.

Under considerable pressure from the Bangladeshi government, the Foreign and Commonwealth Office behaved entirely appropriately, pointing out the BBC's editorial independence and responsibility, firmly declining to mediate between the BBC External Services and Bangladesh, and directing all complaints to the people responsible for the alleged inaccuracies – ourselves.

There have been other instances of tension when the pressure on the British government has come from a more urgent supplicant than President Ershad. I refer to complaints from President Mohamed Siad Barre who wanted the Somali Service closed – though his government's Information Department urged strongly and contrarily that it should not be – and similar complaints from President Moi of Kenya. In a speech on 24 January 1988 the President counselled his audience 'not to listen to such malicious propaganda machines as the BBC, because whatever they put out about Kenya was uninformed, distorted and bluntly malicious'. He stopped well short – so far as I know – of anything like a call for the closure of the Swahili Service.

Let us examine the dilemma facing the government on occasions such as this, for it is a dilemma: they want to enjoy the credit of paying for a respected international news service; yet they don't want the broadcasts which are supposed to bring approval for Britain to generate disapproval. If the latter consideration outweighs the former, then complaints from the President of Azania can be answered in the way he desires – by closing the offending service. One problem would be solved but others would be created – of a far more serious kind. Firstly, the British government would have been seen to interfere with an institution whose independence it regularly proclaims. Secondly, all previous government statements on the subject would be exposed as merely convenient rather than truthful. Thirdly, there would be a queue of leaders asking for similar summary executions. Fourthly, it would fatally undermine the credibility of the External Services and would confirm the persistent claims of detractors that, in the last resort, the government pays the piper and if the piper's tune is too disagreeable, then he will be told to shut up.

Such would be the price of appeasing the President of Azania. What would be gained except a temporary quiet life? The government would have assuaged the sensitivities of a ruler who usually has a great deal to be sensitive about, controls his local media and resents his inability to control those from outside. Invariably, the nature of the political threats he is facing are far more powerful than the voice of the BBC alone. We report the symptoms; we can never be the cause. Usually politics will have their way; silencing the BBC will not save such a ruler.

So can a government derive any benefits from sticking to the publicly articulated line that broadcasting credibility – like peace – is indivisible? That you take the rough with the smooth. I believe they can and that the benefits spring both from immediate policy considerations as well as from deeper considerations of principle.

The policy considerations are both positive and negative. The negative benefit – if you can have such a thing – accrues from not undermining the principle of broadcasting independence which the government's ministers and ambassadors publicly assert. The positive benefit derives from having demonstrated the proclaimed independence in action. Britain gained from reporting the struggle against Amin in Uganda because the insurgents perceived the reports as being in their favour. The reports were not slanted towards them but when political events go your way then you tend to see journalists as supporters of your cause. Similarly, the independent government of Bangladesh perceived BBC reporting as having been in favour of their struggle and against the attempt of the unitary government of Pakistan to preserve the country's unity.

Such instances may appear uncontentious – who, it could be asked, was in favour of Amin? Who was in favour of Ayub Khan's attempt in the mid-1960s to suppress Sheikh Mujibur Rahman's Awami League in East Pakistan (as it then was)? However, there are many only slightly less malodorous regimes whose continuation is seen, at one time or another, to be in the British government's interest. Governments often cannot choose their bedfellows. The consistent reporting of their actions in full detail, regardless of the political consequences and occasional inconvenience, is likely to produce a rather greater long-term benefit to

Britain than backing a regime which ultimately proves unworthy of support.

Long-term principle argues far more strongly in favour of consistent and credible reporting, whatever the short-term disadvantages. That principle is simply the belief in free speech and free communication and is not quite as self-evident as it may sound at first hearing. It is extremely difficult to have a stable, orderly, and peacefully self-regulating international order without free and accurate international communications. Nations cannot – and do not – deal with each other honestly at the conference table if the airwaves are thick with virulent denunciation, distortion, personal denigration and discrediting of motives. If a state only tells its people lies about its antagonists it is that much harder – though not impossible – to switch from one policy to another. If a state negotiates with another, claims good faith, and all the while execrates the negotiating partner in its broadcasts, then its own good faith is in some doubt.

Free international broadcasting is a token of a state's commitment to decent, trustworthy international conduct. If the British government were to prevent the External Services from reporting unpalatable facts, the net result would be to degrade the international information environment to the level of our ideological opponents. By standing up for the principle of international broadcasting freedom, even when it is temporarily inconvenient in short-term policy matters, the government takes a step towards the kind of international communications environment in which harmonious relations between states have a chance of developing. At this point the approach of academe and the demands of principle in foreign policy come to a positive resolution. The balance is achieved because the contradictions are removed.

Yet before deciding that there is no fundamental long-term contradiction between our conflicting responsibilities to academe and government, let us consider the proposition that the External Services, far from being detached from governmental values, should be far closer to them. This was a subject debated in some detail by the Commons Select Committee on Foreign Affairs in 1987. Its particular theme was that of 'cultural diplomacy', a hybrid term for a hybrid concept. I prefer 'alternative diplomacy', a term which acknowledges that the two principal institutions involved in this activity – ourselves and the British Council – clearly aim to raise Britain's image abroad and to gain credit, win prestige and improve the perception of the country from which we come, whose values we reflect, and whose interests are ours. Yet because we are not diplomats, and because we do not reflect the short-term policy interests of the government of the day, our 'para-diplomatic' activities put us at a distance from, though usually in a direction parallel to, our diplomats. Very often Britain gains more official and public credit from the activities of the British Council and the BBC than it does from the activities of diplomats. That is a comment on their task and not on their capability. They have to manage relations between governments; we articulate relations between peoples; the latter is rather easier than the former.

The Commons Select Committee did assert some fundamental principles. It recognised cultural diplomacy as something at which Britain is rather good; it praised our two principal institutions for this purpose; and it called on government to recognise the value of their independence and the benefits which would accrue if they were more ambitiously funded.

The Report also made the point that broadcasting was not a tool of foreign policy but a legitimate and successful operation in its own right. The MPs went on to recommend that more should be spent on the propagation of values. The FCO, they reported, had 'failed to convince us that a figure of between 27 and 33 per cent of FCO Diplomatic Funds should be considered the correct proportion to be spent on cultural diplomacy', and they recommended that the government increase the available resources for cultural diplomacy in line with its importance as a central element of Britain's diplomatic effort.

In reply, the government rejected all the Select Committee's careful nuancing and related policy proposals. They took their stand on the unvarnished proposition that all these activities were part of the diplomatic activity of Britain: 'The underlying purposes of diplomacy are the same through whatever medium they may be engaged.' The reply bracketed the Central Office of Information (COI) and the External Services together as if they were the same in role and in institutional definition. And they rejected any attempt to make distinctions: 'We would go further to suggest that it is not realistic to seek a clear dividing line between cultural diplomacy and other forms of diplomacy.' In short, all activities funded by the Foreign Office were swept into one bag – diplomatic – and one embracing activity – diplomacy. All the distinctions that have been refined over a generation, all the lessons about foreign perceptions of the role of the Foreign Office, all the intricate editorial case-law which has won for the External Services the editorial freedom and managerial responsibility which are the necessary conditions of our credibility, were swept aside. There is – according to this view – no middle ground.

But then that is the difference between academe and Whitehall. The immediate principle demands that public spending shall not increase. There is therefore no point in devising new departmental policies which conflict with this over-riding governmental principle. It is a principle which does not regard the funding of departmental policies – however admirable – as a priority call on national revenues. 'This government is revenue-driven, and not policy-driven,' it was put to me recently. It explains in part the FCO's refusal to countenance approving, defining and then attempting to fund the new policy line which was opened out to them by the Foreign Affairs Committee Report. We could be the most efficient broadcasters in the world, satisfy every inquiry by the Treasury or the National Audit Office and still be bad broadcasters. We should be efficient; we try to be. But first we have to be good broadcasters. We cannot be driven by revenue considerations, though we are limited by revenue constraints. In this – as in so many other matters – we find ourselves far closer to the values of academe than to those of government.

This chapter was first delivered as 'Between Academe & Foreign Policy – the Work of the BBC's External Services' at the London School of Economics Seminar on 2 February 1988.

FREEDOM AND RESPONSIBILITY IN BROADCASTING

When we discuss the media, that unlovely collective noun coined to embrace both the print and electronic media, we are of course dealing with power. Like a set of subscription channels in a cable or satellite system, the components of the media cannot be as simply unbundled as Lord Chalfont has appeared to imply [at the Seminar where this essay was first delivered in spoken form]. Any examination of the social impact of public forms of communication will go seriously astray if it concentrates on one and ignores the other, taking the view that consumers have a choice when it comes to print but suffer radio and television under compulsion. If the reader wants a quality daily newspaper, he or she has a selection of five (*not* an unlimited choice). On television, he or she has a choice of six channels: four formal channels and two informal ones; those two comprising one channel showing the products of the video shops, and another showing programmes recorded from the four main channels and then viewed in displaced time. Such a picture hardly supports the attempt to put broadcasters' problems on a different plane because they do not, allegedly, operate in an area of choice. Apart from anything else, the on/off button is surely an instrument of choice.

While we are about it, let us look at another of Lord Chalfont's questionable assumptions: the relationship between words and images in television. The assertion that the 'words are peripheral or at best secondary' would be challenged by any serious practitioner in the television industry and sits oddly with the fact that many of the major political *causes célèbres* of television have turned on the words as much as the images.

But what we are discussing is an age-old dilemma. Gilbert argued with Sullivan over it. And Richard Strauss wrote an entire opera about it. Which comes first, the words or the music? 'Prima la musica, dopo le parole.' At the end of Strauss's *Capriccio*, the Countess agrees to choose between the poet and the composer in the drawing-room the following morning at 11. How does she choose? Strauss's music supplies the answer. I invite Lord Chalfont to entertain the proposition that words and images on television are integrated in an altogether more complex, more subtle, and less simplistic way than he has asserted and that the debate is best conducted (as Gilbert and Sullivan and Strauss did) with a mature recognition that there is no black and white answer.

So, having discounted the assumption that problems exist only in the electronic media, let us return to the question of power and the fear and loathing – that is a phrase, not a charge – that goes with it.

It is March 1923. John Reith, Managing Director of the British Broadcasting Company, has invited the Archbishop of Canterbury and Mrs Randall Davidson to dinner. Reith is demonstrating the wonders of the wireless to his guests who ask him if it was necessary to open the windows to hear it? There was no piano solo on the air that evening and the Archbishop particularly wished to hear one. Reith rang up and got them to play Schubert's 'Marche Militaire'. The Archbishop was 'entirely amazed, thunderstruck indeed'. Two years later in March 1925 Prime Minister Stanley Baldwin and Reith were discussing power in the modern community. Baldwin said he had been conscious of it when, late for an official engagement, he had been driven down the wrong side of Piccadilly. Reith replied that he could pick up his phone, say 'SB' which would connect him to the control room and all the BBC transmitters, and he could then talk to several million people. Baldwin agreed that this implied greater power than his car exploit. We do not use these inventions as playthings today. So how much freedom do we have, and how much responsibility do we display as broadcasters?

Let me attempt to dispel – though with no very lively hopes of success (as Sidney Smith once commented to John Wilkes when he said he was going to St Paul's to pray for him) – the prevalent view of the broadcasting journalist as a lawless unprincipled egotist, unrestrained by editors, and utterly unconcerned about the consequences of his or her actions. I speak from a position of working in and around and for the BBC – by no means the same thing – for 28 years. I have had too the opportunity of working for substantial periods of time in all three Directorates – External, Radio and Television – as a journalist on the current affairs and documentary side. I do not claim that I or my colleagues begin every day by thinking about the observation made by the novelist P. H. Newby, then Head of the Third Programme, in 1965: 'The healthy attitude for anyone working in the mass media is one of fear and trembling.' But producers have a healthy awareness of their responsibility to the society which has given them a key place in the major institutions of public information. They feel a duty to society as a whole rather than to the government of the day. And that duty consists of reporting events, reflecting opinions and examining ideas. The precise combination of those activities varies according to the nature of the programme. But their purpose is always to provide citizens with as full, accurate and informed a picture of events as a democratic society needs to operate in a flexibly articulated way.

Few producers would, I hope, have any difficulty with the description offered by Charles Curran in his book, *The Seamless Robe*:

> *The BBC as an institution is the child of parliamentary democracy. And the whole concept of its establishment assumes its support of that system. I once heard one of the BBC's senior editors admit that we were biased. 'Yes,' he said, 'biased in favour of parliamentary democracy.' And he was absolutely right. That form of democracy depends on there being a plurality of opinions, on the freedom of their expression, on their public dissemination, and on the resolution, in circumstances of tolerance, of the differences of view which will then arise. The resolution for the time being of those differences is embodied at any given moment in the current policy of the prevailing government. It is a matter of accommodation, of tolerance, not of principle. No public policy is 'right'. It is simply accepted for the time being. Democracy allows for the possibility of change and for the possibility of argument for it.*

Does this amount to power, let alone unbridled power? It

certainly points to a challenging responsibility. Most broadcasters would react to the idea of their possessing great power as did Desmond Taylor, a former BBC Editor of News and Current Affairs, in a BBC lecture in 1975:

> *When I was first told that I held a position of great power, my reaction was incredulity – I have never had a sense of power and this is a common reaction among broadcasters. If I have power, I asked myself, I must be able to exercise it, yet I know that if I tried with whatever skill and cunning to make Communists vote Conservative, or to make everybody drink milk, nothing would happen – except that people in the BBC would soon realise what was going on and I wouldn't be allowed to get away with it. To approach the proposition another way, I thought of things that really have influenced men's minds, like King James's Bible and John Bunyan's Pilgrim's Progress. When I added D. Taylor to that list, I found the result comical.*

So far, so easy. In practice, broadcast journalism is far from easy and often difficult. It requires courage. In January 1938, the BBC Arabic Service went on the air, the result of a government decision that the tide of Italian propaganda in the Arab world required a counterbalance. The very first bulletin carried the news of the execution by the British authorities of a Palestinian Arab found guilty of carrying a gun. Rex Leeper, then Head of the Foreign Office News Department, was affronted and expressed his displeasure in no uncertain terms. Fortunately J. B. Clark, then Director of the Empire Service, stood firmly by the principle of accurate and impartial reporting at all times.

In 1956 during the Suez Crisis, a similar position was maintained by the BBC in the face of a far greater crisis and far greater criticism from the government of the day under Anthony Eden. Writing after the event the Director-General, Sir Ian Jacob, observed:

> *If the BBC is found for the first time to be suppressing significant items of news, its reputation would rapidly vanish and the harm to the national interest done in the event would enormously outweigh any damage caused by displaying to the*

world the workings of a free democracy. If there is to be a censorship of adverse opinion then it must be exercised at the source by the government. It cannot be exercised by the Corporation.

J. B. Clark, Sir Ian Jacob and countless others carried the responsibility for taking a decision that went counter to the wishes of the government of the day. They were free to take the opposite decision. But they acted responsibly in taking the one that they did. I would not want you to think that such confrontation is the inevitable staple of relations between government and broadcasters or that governments are always bent on imposing their will. In the somewhat unlikely times of 1943, Brendan Bracken, then Minister of Information, made this statement about the relationship between broadcasters and the authorities:

Some people think there is a great mystery between the Ministry of Information and the BBC . . . I shall attempt to pierce that mystery. At the beginning of this war the government were given power to interfere in the affairs of every institution in this country including the BBC. And though I am always willing to take responsibility for all the BBC's doings, I have refused to interfere in the policies of the Corporation. The Governors and many members of the staff often consult with the Ministry of Information and sometimes they condescend to ask us for our advice and we give it for what it is worth. But I can say from my own personal experience that no attempt has ever been made by the government to influence the news-giving or any other programme of the BBC. In fact, I am constantly advising my friends in the BBC of the desirability of being independent and of being very tough with anyone who attempts to put pressure upon you.

Ultimately, journalists have no alternative but to bear the responsibility placed upon them – to act as primary conduits of news, events and ideas to the listening and watching public. But because a particular duty is inherent in an activity, there is no guarantee that it will be exercised responsibly. Let us look at four cases of the exercise of responsibility in very different circumstances. Three affect the External Services and one other international media.

The first occurred in 1967. The then Foreign Secretary, George Brown, was in Moscow for negotiations about the situation in the Middle East: Israel and her Arab neighbours were on the verge of war. The Soviet Union made it clear that if the BBC Russian Service went ahead with its planned serialisation of Svetlana Stalin's *Letters to a Friend* they would regard it as an unfriendly act and the negotiations would be placed in jeopardy.

There was much discussion between Downing Street, the Foreign Office and the BBC. The upshot was that the Director-General, Sir Hugh Greene, decided that it would not be right for the BBC to pretend to be a judge in a matter of national interest involving peace and war. The programme was deferred and transmitted 48 hours later.

The second example concerns Uganda. It was in 1975. A journalist called David Martin, who had worked as a reporter for the BBC in East Africa, had written a frank book on Idi Amin. The British High Commission in Kampala judged that any interview with David Martin that the BBC planned to broadcast would endanger the lives of British citizens in Uganda. Bearing in mind the record of Idi Amin, his proven unpredictability and ferocity, the BBC agreed to postpone the programme. We did not feel it was for us to put lives at risk. The interview was broadcast three weeks later on our own initiative without informing the Foreign and Commonwealth Office. We had satisfied ourselves that there would be no repercussions and there were none. I should add that when we discussed this event in early 1987 at a senior editorial meeting, the man responsible for deciding to delay the interview regretted having done so. He regarded it as a false exercise of responsibility, and felt that in holding back information about Uganda – albeit not of an essential kind – we had not kept faith with our audience who expect us to play straight.

There is a third instance. During the Soviet invasion of Hungary in 1956 some Western radio stations gave listeners in that country an unrealistic picture of the reaction of the NATO powers. The insurgents were led to believe that help would soon be on its way. Encouragement was given to mount further resistance, and many lives were uselessly lost.

The BBC Hungarian Service and the World Service took a clear decision about coverage. While conveying fully the sympathy and the horror of the world outside at what was happening in Budapest, it gave a sober and factual analysis of the international situation. It did not raise false hopes. It brought comfort when it could, but it never concealed the harsh reality, nor the likely outcome.

A further instance where the responsibility of broadcasters was called into question, was coverage of the so-called Palestinian Uprising. (Incidentally, we refused to call it 'the Uprising' for many weeks because that was the title which the PLO had given it and we judged that to use the title in the early days would constitute a political comment.) The coverage of the Palestinian riots raised a question almost as old as the words and music argument – cause and effect in political coverage. At a convention of the National Association of Broadcasters in Las Vegas in 1988, the issue was confronted directly by the President of NBC News, Larry Grossmann. He was asked whether the national press should be expected to operate in the national interest. Provocatively, Grossmann said 'No,' and for the following reasons:

The press is not qualified and has no standing to decide what the national interest is, and whether that interest might ever justify the suppression of information. Even the government's view of what is in the national interest is often mistaken and distorted by its concern for its own self-preservation. That is why in times of crisis, truth is usually the first casualty.

In times of crisis, there are just two questions the reporter or editor should ask. Is the story true? And, will it help the reader or viewer judge the actions and policies of his government? If the answer to both those questions is yes, then there is no reason for either restraint or self-censorship.

Grossmann then went on to distinguish between national interest and national security and asserted that he knew of no responsible journalist who ever actually violated national security even though, as Justice Brennan of the Supreme Court had noted, 'the perceived threats to national security that have motivated the sacrifice of civil liberties during times of crisis are often overblown and factually unfounded'. Grossmann concluded:

In times of trouble, we tend to dwell on television's capacity to undermine national unity and public morale. And in truth, where there is no national consensus, television does tend to highlight public dissent and political differences. Television is thought to be good when it shows consensus . . . the image of Sadat in Jerusalem, the signing of the Camp David accords. Television is considered bad when it shows troubles and disturbances, when it seems to stimulate national controversy. The job of the press is not to worry about the consequences of its coverage, but to tell the truth. Freedom of the press is really nothing more than our protection against sweeping key problems under the rug. Television's coverage enables us, indeed compels us to confront painful issues first-hand. As much as those of us in the press would like to be popular and loved, it is more important that we are accurate and fair . . . and let the chips fall where they may.

That is the ultimate responsibility of the press in a democratic society.

We are of course talking about drawing lines and in this context it might be a good idea to look at an extreme view of journalistic activity. I am not suggesting that this is the model critics of present-day journalism want in any way to impose but it may be useful in securing a baseline for discussion. This extreme view operates with monotonous regularity in most closed societies though it seems to be starting to change slightly. In closed societies there is little doubt as to where the responsibility of the journalist lies. In Communist states it is to the Party, as the directing force in the state.

Lenin enunciated the maxims which have guided the conduct of the Soviet writer and broadcaster since the revolution. Revolutionary journalism, according to Lenin, meant that the writers (and therefore the broadcasters) 'must constantly work as publicists and write the history of our time'.

This branch of the intellectual élite should:

try to write in such a way that our chronicles do what they can to help the direct participants in the movement and the proletarian heroes there, at the scene of the action; write in such a way as to facilitate the expansion of the movement and a conscious choice of the means, ways, and methods of struggle capable of producing the greatest and most durable results with the smallest effort.

In short, the press was to be 'a serious organ for the economic education for the masses of the population'.

Elements of this kind of thinking lay behind the attempts to create the New World Information Order in the United Nations Educational, Scientific and Cultural Organisation (UNESCO). This effort to circumscribe the work of reporters, to ensure that their copy took on a more 'constructive' tone, has, after a strenuous campaign in the Western press, been laid to rest. However, it attracted a surprisingly wide degree of support in the developing world, because many politicians in those countries were, and are, apprehensive of the power of the Western media: the news agencies like Reuters, United Press International (UPI), Associated Press (AP); the international radio networks such as the Voice of America, Deutsche Welle and the BBC; and now the growth of television channels such as Cable News Network beamed around the globe by satellite.

Third World politicians saw their countries reported 'irresponsibly' by the media; that is to say, not with the interests of the developing countries in mind but with stories shaped to appeal to audiences in New York or London or Frankfurt. The Third World was reported in terms of disaster and coups, starvation and assassination. There was a lack of 'positive' stories. The New World Information Order was a somewhat clumsy attempt to remedy that state of affairs.

One must admit that these states do have a poor press – they do tend to be reported in sensationalist terms. The stereotype is often reinforced to the extent that the listener/viewer/reader in Atlantica comes to think of Africa, Asia and Latin America as hopeless 'here be dragons' space on the map. So in the draft of the UNESCO Paper on Information there was a phrase calling for a 'free and balanced flow of information'. The word 'balanced' has been criticised in the West for its implication that some deliberate 'correction' is being applied when stories are filed, that there is some manipulation at the editing stage. In fact it was a code word indicating that some positive official claims should be set against the apparently 'pessimistic' reports of outside correspondents. It contained no sense that the good news should be tested – as the bad news was – against reality. In fact it called for special pleading in coverage of the Third World and it was rightly resisted. The problem might perhaps be ameliorated if bad news was reported in a less doom-laden, sensationalist way.

We are not discussing here the Leninist view and the Third World view of the journalist as the functionary of the state. But I do confess that I grow uneasy when I hear that journalists do not promote the values of the 'enterprise culture' sufficiently. The argument is that they come from a culture – liberal, arts presumably – which is congenitally and intellectually incapable of evaluating the achievements of an enterprise culture and so may be disqualified from commenting on, still less criticising, that culture. In 1968 Tony Benn complained that television was not telling the nation enough about the white heat of Harold Wilson's scientific revolution, and that the whole container revolution had gone by without adequate coverage and explanation. More than 20 years on, that demand for a special commitment from journalists to a particular set of policies sounds as dated as the desired commitment to the enterprise culture may seem two decades from now. Whatever the answers to our problems, they do not lie in that direction.

And let us be fair to Lenin. He did call for reportage of successes but only if there were real successes to report:

> *Are they proven? Are they tales, bragging and intellectual promises, e.g. 'it's being organised', 'a plan is being drawn up', 'we are mobilising our forces', 'the improvement is indisputable' and other such charlatan phrases at which 'we' are such experts . . . Where is the list of backward factories, examples of disorder, disarray, filth, hooliganism and parasitism?*
> *There isn't one, but such factories do exist.*

And as authoritative voices such as Academician Abel Agan-begyan told his audiences in Britain in 1987, for decades Soviet statistics and Soviet journalists paraded and flaunted figures which were not simply a little bit short of the truth, they were miles away. So if the role of the responsible journalist is not as a chamberlain to the government, what should he or she be?

Let us recall the information context in which the journalist works. Firstly, there is the Official Secrets Act which even distinguished former Sir Humphrey Applebys agree stifles the flow of quantities of essential public information. Secondly, there is the government information machine. It calculates how the news is to be revealed, when it is to be revealed, what part of it is to be revealed and often to whom it will be revealed. It uses a panoply of official and unofficial briefings, attributable and unattributable quotes, lobbies, news conferences, interviews and television advertisements to convey this information. It is a formidable array of human and financial resources designed to put over the government's case.

How should the responsible journalist react? First, as a conduit of information. The government has a right to be heard, the public a right to hear what has been said. Second, as a critic, not in the subjective sense that I may not like your tie or may dislike the performance of an opera, but in the objective sense of a trained observer who uses his or her mind, knowledge and experience to subject the government's claims and policies to the kind of scrutiny that the average citizen would want to give if they had the time and the expertise. The journalist as critic is the agent of the audience. Nobody feels qualified to make up their minds on all the subjects that appear in the press and television. We need the journalist critic to act on our behalf, to look behind and beyond the claims of government. For all policies are by their nature mere claims, not certainties. They will be tested – often to destruction – by reality and time. The task of the responsible journalist is to be an early part of that process, and if the result is unpopular, then responsibility demands that you face that unpopularity with chapter and verse.

But there is another, more fundamental role for responsible broadcasters to play – as a sounding-board for ideas in society. Here is a small personal instance to demonstrate the process I have in mind. In 1968 I was preparing a filmed report on housing for the *Money Programme*. We included contributions from economists at the Institute for Economic Affairs who argued for a massive increase of the private rented sector as the only way of solving the housing crisis. Such were neither orthodox ideas nor popular ones. The Labour Housing Minister complained most strongly at the very inclusion of such heterodox stuff. A couple of decades later, they are part of the new orthodoxy. How did ideas like those, and many others from the new liberalism, become the prevalent intellectual currency of the land except by broadcasters acting as a conduit for thought and ideas? Such a process will always be unpopular with the custodians of the prevailing new orthodoxy. In this respect only, I agree with the Marxist analysis. I believe in the dialectic of ideas, that every one produces its own antithesis and the seeds of its own change or destruction, because reality and experience themselves alter and challenge ideas in the light of events.

It is the duty of responsible journalists to be at the heart of this process, not as personalised agents of change, but as instruments whereby ideas are transmitted. Broadcasters are bound by their professional responsibilities as journalists and as people who wield influence – perhaps sometimes power – in a confused and agitated world. The freedom they exercise is the freedom to be responsible. Beyond that, the danger of calls for more responsibility is that they are code words for self-censorship, for obliging accommodation with the government of the day, for acceptance of the prevailing governmental culture. Journalists must not be the outriders of authority.

This chapter was first delivered as 'The Problems of Freedom and Responsibility in Broadcasting' at the Sir Huw Wheldon Bangor Fellowship Inaugural Seminar, University College of North Wales on 25 June 1988.

CHALLENGING
THE CENSORS

Britain may have less censorship than some other countries but few – if any – British journalists believe that our news environment is as free as it should be. The Official Secrets Act continues to prowl its maverick way through the information thickets of Whitehall, living up to its description as 'a blunderbuss' which, when brought out of the armoury, usually does as much damage to the user as the intended victim. We also have the Edwardian beauties of the lobby system where – and here I express myself in an entirely personal capacity – the unmentionable opinion is authorised by the unattributable source for the inadmissible reason. In this way, any political gentleman – or lady – can speak ill of another through their *éminences grises* and then deny that they ever said it. Trial balloons, calculated leaks, misleading steers – these are all part of what is laughingly called the British official information process.

In some respects the whole operation is harmless enough. After all, when you and I read that a 'Downing Street source' has said this or that, we all know who it is. 'Sources close to the Prime Minister', 'Sources at the highest level', 'It can be said on the highest authority' – all can be, and have been, used as ill-concealed code words for a quiet word with the boss him or herself. You know it; I know it; but do they, our readers, viewers and listeners, know it? Probably not. Because the whole Whitehall convention of coded information is not an attempt to conceal; it is rather a massive tribute to British snobbery, the élitist idea that we are in the know but they aren't. Knowledge is power and we're going to keep it that way. In some respects it's all quite harmless. But the joke does rebound on us – for in the end we only fool ourselves.

That same belief – that knowledge is power – has spawned far more venomous progeny in countries less fundamentally tolerant than ours. In such countries censorship is operated and, as with all such challenges, instantly prompts a determination to break it.

Gordon Martin, the BBC External Services Diplomatic correspondent, was in Cairo some years ago when a Soviet aircraft was shot down. It was officially confirmed by President Sadat himself, though the censor – clearly a prudent man – banned all reports. However, Reuter did get one take of the story through before the wires were cut. So, where was the confirming source which would allow us to carry this major story? Gordon used his wit. He sent a personal telegram to a friend in Bush House saying simply 'Trust the baron', relying on his friend to recall that Julius Reuter was himself a baron. On the strength of this we broadcast the report, and the censorship was immediately lifted.

In Nigeria, during the overthrow of the Prime Minister Sir Abubakar Tafawa Balewa, Angus McDermid avoided censorship by filing to Bush House in Welsh. What is truly remarkable is that there was someone there who could decode it.

Again, during the 1967 Middle East War our correspondent in Saudi Arabia, Tony Dunn, aware of the sensitivities of the story and the crushing counter-attack of the Israelis, decided the only sure way to get his message over was to file in Swahili. He was secure in the knowledge that Bush House could easily translate it.

Sometimes the best way to avoid censorship is by hitching a ride. In Ghana, our then Commonwealth Correspondent was in a position to report the widespread ballot rigging of general elections. As all phones to London were mysteriously out of order, Andrew Walker sent a recorded cassette to London via a willing pigeon – a friendly civilian carrier – and then wisely departed in the opposite direction, knowing he would be very unpopular in Ghana when his report broke.

In Buenos Aires during the Falklands War, Harold Briley, our Defence Correspondent, witnessed the problems that BBC television faced in not having access to satellites back to London. When London received the code message, 'We're going by clog tonight', it indicated that BBC material was being sent over on the tail-end of the Dutch satellite.

And on the subject of codes, a traditional way of informing the newsroom that a dispatch has been sent under censorship is to say 'Give my love to Norma'. Unfortunately Harold Briley's wife is called Norah and all his attempts to alert London to the censorship, led only to repeated promises that they would of course phone his wife and pass on his love.

Such experiences are the stock in trade of all journalists. But in broadcasting we are vulnerable to a particularly noxious form of censorship – you might call it censorship at the point of use – jamming. Here the censor doesn't just cut out particular stories, or particular pieces of information. He shuts the whole lot out. Whole world views are judged so damaging that they cannot be allowed in. We must be very powerful if we are considered to be so dangerous.

As far as the Soviet Union is concerned, our Russian language broadcasts were jammed from 1949 to 1963. Then, following a period of relaxation, jamming was reimposed after the Soviet invasion of Czechoslovakia in 1968. That phase lasted five years, to be followed by a further seven years of free transmission. In 1980 jamming started again on 20 August and continued until 21 January 1987. Our Polish Service transmissions in short wave were jammed by the Russians until 1 January 1988.

We in the BBC are of course not the only targets of Soviet jamming; there are other broadcasts such as Radio Liberty, Radio Free Europe, Voice of America, Deutsche Welle and Kol Israel, which have also been blotted out, and at an extraordinary cost. BBC estimates are that the whole operation – including local jamming of signals into urban areas of more than 100 000 people; sky wave jamming and monitoring and control of the jamming signal – could cost as much as £626 million per year. The Soviet Union is the only place in the world where the country bumpkin is better informed than the city slicker.

Whichever country you are in, censorship has a thousand faces, openness only one. Of all its masks, self-censorship – the willing decision not to report something you know is happening – can be as bad as any. Sometimes the very distinction between objective and subjective reality can be thrown into question. I was once in a prosperous village in North China – the cameraman and director were shooting a sequence of donkeys pulling carts. Nothing very remarkable but, by the standards of that particular location, reasonably picturesque. Our official party cadre guide took exception.

'Why are you always filming donkeys?' he asked irritably.

'Because they are there,' we replied, or some such.

'No,' he insisted, 'you should not be filming them. They are not important.'

'What do you mean?' we asked.

'Because,' he explained, 'soon they will be tractors.'

In South Africa today of course we have a particularly glaring case of 'ostrich censorship' – that is to say the belief that if you can prevent people seeing something happening then either it isn't happening or it will actually go away. Philosophically this view – not confined to the authorities in South Africa – holds (argues is not the word) that the report of the event serves to create it, an Alice in Wonderland view of cause and effect that only a censor could believe.

My favourite instance of this belief in action occurred in 1985 when BBC journalists went on strike in protest at the decision by the BBC Governors (following representations by government) not to transmit a programme about political extremists in Northern Ireland. On the day of the strike *The Times* carried a triumphant letter from a bishop, no less. It included these confident words: 'From this mass of hysteria [the NUJ strike] we can gain one solid crumb of comfort. No IRA members will commit murder on Wednesday because there will be a total blackout of news.' And he suggested – as an episcopal jest, no doubt – that if the screens were blank for a week, then there would be a week without IRA murders. But then he was a man of faith.

Years ago a BBC reporter was on the streets of Belfast when rioting and mayhem broke out all round him. His cameraman was calmly recording the scene in all its lurid orange and green detail when an irate local citizen came up, thrust her fist over the lens and delivered herself of the immortal verdict: 'You are showing things that aren't even happening.' Which could be the motto of the official censor down the ages. To which all we can say is: 'Would that we were.'

This chapter was first delivered as 'Challenging the Censors' at the World News Media Action Conference on 16 January 1987.

CHANGING AN INSTITUTION – THE NEW-LOOK WORLD SERVICE

Nobody tampers with an institution lightly. The BBC World Service is an institution and we have tampered with it. Do we deserve to be let off lightly? According to a sizeable clutch of correspondents, no sentence would be too harsh. 'In my opinion,' wrote one from Australia, 'you have perpetrated change for change's sake ... It's like putting the Queen into pink tights at her birthday parade with the massed bands playing Satchmo tunes while jiggling, US college band style.' Another, writing from Britain, quoted Caius Petronius, who wrote in AD 66: 'We tend to meet any new situation by reorganising, and a wonderful method it can be for creating the illusion of progress while producing confusion, inefficiency, and demoralisation.' That, he said, was what we had done to the World Service. Others were less temperate and if they had known a *fatwa* before the Ayatollah had brought it so brutally into the contemporary idiom with his sentence on Salman Rushdie, would undoubtedly have urged an arrow to speed itself towards my heart.

What have we done to the World Service? Why have we done it? And were we wise to start? Perhaps it is worth saying that the changes so passionately criticised by some listeners were designed to improve the service, not to vandalise it. They include a new 60-minute news and current affairs programme called *Newshour*, widening the range of our current affairs coverage. (It has, incidentally, been warmly praised by every radio critic who has reviewed it.) They also include an extra edition of *Newsdesk*, an editorially improved *Newsreel*, expanded financial news to give better round-the-clock coverage, a new weekly round-up of world events called *World Brief*, and a new general interest magazine programme for younger listeners called *Megamix*. Beyond that, regular programmes were carefully scrutinised and reviewed to see if their working assumptions were soundly based. Some were subtly shifted, others left alone. There was no change for change's sake but only change where it was required. In all, the new programmes added to the proportion of news and current affairs on the network and slightly reduced that of pop music.

Certain things were left untouched: 'Lilliburlero'; 'Big Ben'; the 9-minute news bulletin; the quality of English speaking. One new Scottish-accented newsreader quickly established herself as a favourite with a fan club around the world.

But why did we feel the need to change anything in what was already regarded as the world's best and most reliable news network? There were both strategic and tactical reasons for believing that change was needed. These led to the commissioning of research. And the research pointed to areas where change could usefully be introduced.

The first strategic reason sprang from a study of the comments usually made about the former World Service. It was praised because it was good at its job, but also because it was old-fashioned. Some listeners loved the plummy voices, the long pauses between sentences, the measured tones, the sheer oddity of it all. One correspondent wrote that the signature tunes were so outdated that 'they were if anything intentionally retro-chic'. Another correspondent, Myles Harris, writing in the *Spectator*, praised: 'old-fashioned, upper-class announcers, a stiff delivery and a series of sometimes uproariously quirky programmes'.

Such praise of oddity, of eccentricity, sounded a deep warning signal to me. A network cannot be good, excellent and admired, and comic at the same time. Unless this image was shed, the balance between those who thought it good and slightly eccentric and those who mainly found it only eccentric would tip disastrously. As a piece of 'brand positioning', it was fraught with peril. Those who admired the Service for its oddity were principally engaging in an eccentric indulgence of their own. It was only a short step from that to not being taken seriously at all. So the principal tactical reason was the need to avoid ossification. There were some in Bush House who resolutely opposed changes on grounds that had been respectable 20 years ago but had not changed since. They were not tablets of stone but sacred cows. And these sacred cows were in danger of running out of milk.

The next stage was to verify these instinctive judgements with research. It was by no means clear that the research would indeed verify them, and it was not commissioned in order to endorse our working assumptions.

Earlier research conducted between 1986 and 1987 in six countries had asked correspondents to describe the BBC World Service as a person. These were some of the responses: 'conservative, not too exciting, does not like changes', 'the aunt who is at times very serious, at times very funny, a bit whimsical', 'ponderous, informed, erudite. Not much of a sense of humour. I'd be glad to know that person'. That research noted that correspondents liked much of what they heard of news and current affairs 'although a more relaxed tone might be appreciated elsewhere in the output'.

In March 1987, an internal World Service committee reported on the sound of the Service. The results were not flattering, and included the following comments: 'The sound is ten years out of date in UK terms', 'World Service sound is the natural extension of the way we are organised. We are organised badly', 'Quaintness and clunks are not contemporary', 'Comings and goings, disembodied voices not acknowledging each other'. It was all summed up in one sentence: 'I think we have a problem here.'

That survey produced compelling evidence that, within the organisation itself, there were few supporters of the way the network presented itself to its audience. Such an undertow of negative views revealed the extent to which the presentation had lost credibility at its very source.

Another internal report in 1987 on news and current affairs concluded:

> World Service is informative and educative but too often dull, dutiful and mechanical. There is much respect for news and current affairs programmes, there is also criticism of style and presentation. We do not sound contemporary, we do not sound attractive.

Taken together, these reports pointed to a potentially destructive situation where those who were responsible for World Service journalism in its entirety no longer believed in the way it was being done.

But there was more research to be carried out – about the World Service listener. In January 1988, our International Broadcasting Audience Research Department produced a number of conclusions. Those who listened to us in English numbered 25 million. Of those, World Service listeners were men rather than women; urban rather than rural; young rather than old: well educated rather than poorly educated. And, most of the listeners did *not* have English as a first language. To underline this last point, it was noted that 'Well over eight out of ten British expatriates are in areas which make up less than one in ten of the World Service regular audience'. If it needed underlining, the World Service is not for expatriates and is used predominantly by those who are not expatriates. Indeed, the World Service does best in those regions where English is not spoken widely as a first language. North America holds 40 per cent of the world's English speakers but less than 10 per cent of the World Service audience.

There are warnings, too, or a challenge, if you want to look at it that way: 'World Service seems to have penetrated about 4 per cent of its theoretical potential audience – 9 per cent in sub-Saharan Africa, 8 per cent in Central and South America, but just 1 per cent in North America and Australasia.'

The research then attempted to establish when people tended to listen. We now know that there is a 'developed world curve' and a 'developing world curve'. The former curve – the developed world – has its listening peak in the morning at breakfast time. But the developing world curve has a peak just as large in the evening and almost as large at lunchtime.

Much of this information was new to us. Putting it together with the reports from the internal review panels, the outlines of World Service Renewal took shape. The entire process took some two years and was marked by a large degree of internal agreement about the need for such renewal and about the form it should take.

It was implemented gradually: programmes were reshaped as the opportunity arose; voices were replaced as the opportunity occurred. Much had already been changed, quietly, without fanfare, when it was decided to unveil 'World Service Renewal' to the press in October 1988. All went well except with the reporter from the *Daily Telegraph*. She chose to use the word 'colloquial' to describe the tone of voice being sought from our newsreaders and continuity announcers. It was seized upon by the *Evening Standard* who had not attended the news conference, by the *Daily Mail*, by the *Spectator* and by the *Observer*.

Naturally, the letter-writers took fright and wrote in. They all did, and do, care passionately about the World Service, which is oddly reassuring. But evidently none of them had listened to it recently. What they valued was an *idea* of the World Service, a Platonic essence, and they were incensed by the very idea of this pure essence being violated. 'I fervently wish that Mrs Thatcher could step in and take control,' wrote one. Another thus: 'I deplore the arrogance that leads you to suppose that you know better what is good for people – for which your *confrère* on Radio Three has, hitherto, taken the biscuit.' I was accused of 'idiocy' for wanting to abandon 'Lilliburlero' – which we had no intention of doing. And so on and so on. What was revealing was that the overwhelming majority wrote on the basis of what they had been told would happen rather than on the basis of experience.

Later the approving letters began to come through, based on listening to the output rather than jumping to the wrong conclusions. We restored the signature tune to *Sports Round-up* and had another attempt at an effective signature tune for *Newsreel*. Beyond that, the changes are in place and have proved themselves overwhelmingly. One correspondent wrote from Britain to applaud the changes in the 'hope that you will be able to rid the Service of its antediluvian pedestrian image'.

My second thoughts on the whole process are these. When you tamper with an institution you run a grave risk of having your motives misinterpreted. If you leave an institution untampered with, then it may be admired but it ceases to be used. Lastly, don't tell anyone what you are doing; the anticipation causes the trouble. Next time, we will simply introduce the changes and leave the audience to find out for themselves. If they don't notice, then we must have got it right.

This chapter was first delivered as 'Changing an Institution – the New Look of the World Service' at the Society of Bookmen on 2 March 1989.

IV

TRAVELS WITH A TANDY

'AFRICA ALWAYS WINS'

UGANDA 16–19 OCTOBER 1988

SUNDAY 16 OCTOBER

Uganda is a consistent place – first impressions are reinforced by later ones. In any case, I come bearing a heavy load of apprehension, born of reading V. S. Naipaul's study of irrational violence in Uganda, *In a Free State*. The Entebbe Airport building looks as if the chickens have only recently left, but at least the droppings have been swept away. The buildings are clearly patched up after the ravages of civil war. Officials are ragged but friendly. Even the airport trolleys have been donated by the United Nations – here development begins at the very beginning. Every visitors must change US $150 at the airport. It is a shock to get a grimy, two-inch thick wad of bank notes in return, the merest glimpse of a Weimar-type experience.

Young porters throng round the cases. Each lifts one; each gets 100 Ugandan shillings (two-thirds of a dollar). Eileen Mullen, the BBC Press Officer, hands out BBC T-shirts; one ragged man pleads, 'Sister, give me a pen', and she does. The first National Resistance Army (NRA) checkpoint is outside the airport. The soldiers are curious, very young, but apparently friendly. The second one, nearer Kampala, is in two stages. The first soldier waves us on; the second one is shirty that we were on the verge of driving through. He solemnly inspects our passports before letting us go. There is an undertone of sheer unpredictability.

In Kampala itself, the Sheraton Hotel is a bizarre lighthouse of Western-style living – I don't say civilisation – in an ocean of political unpredictability. The hotel itself is a metaphor for Uganda's present state. Not long ago it was desolate, empty, with bats hanging from the ceilings. Now it is a functioning hotel, but the gaps still show. There is a shopping arcade but no shops in it. The Penthouse Bar and Luxury Restaurant exist in theory but don't serve anyone. The staff have been thoroughly drilled in behaving as if they were at the Miami Sheraton but the effort shows. It is the same with Uganda. There is a resolute attempt to get the façade in place, but what is shoring it up?

Our plane had arrived at Entebbe 2½ hours late. We have been invited to dinner at the Deputy High Commissioner's for 7.30. We finally arrive at 9 pm but it is well worth it. The girl friend of a former BBC-trained man, Ben, looks very passive and docile, out of place even. Sitting at a table together, I ask her what she does – she's a hairdresser. We are talking with others about how much has changed in Uganda since Amin and Obote. Yes, law and order is better; you can't hear gunshots at night; things are running again. Elisabeth Kanyogonya, who came back to be Museveni's speech-writer, and ended up as his ghost-writer, is impressed. I ask the hairdresser, who has been in the capital for longer than most, for her impressions. Suddenly she starts talking: of her four arrests; of accusations that she had contacts with the rebels in the bush; of being beaten up at the police station; of being so sickened by the reek in the prison that she vomited for a day; of saying to the police who were beating her, 'Please kill me and get it over with'; of meeting one of her torturers in the street and of his appalled disappearance; of living behind a house from which the screams of the tortured were clearly audible in the evenings. Others at the table said there were hundreds of stories like these, but from her it sounded as if it was pouring out uncontrollably and was not often aired.

MONDAY 17 OCTOBER

Up at dawn – 6 am. Kampala lies, dew- and mist-covered, in its valleys. Kites and egrets are circling as the sun rises. At 6.20 Catherine Bond, the BBC stringer, collects us in her red-dusted Suzuki to go to Entebbe for an up-country flight to Serote on a one-engined, four-seater plane hired from Bel Air. The NRA checkpoints are easy and relaxed, persuaded by Catherine's press pass, or perhaps it's too early to be nasty.

Uganda is beautiful from 8000 feet, though Entebbe is 3800 to start with. It looks very green, with the long blue arms of Lake Victoria and then Lake Kyoga, and later the Nile dog-legging its way through the landscape. There are few visible roads, though many tracks. Closer to Serote, we see round-roofed straw huts in small clearings. As we drop down, the land has an uncultivated – or at least a neglected – look. Serote is a flying school (the relics of the former East African Community flying school), still, as we discover later, in good working order.

The day starts with a Ugandan tragedy – an Air Uganda 707 crashes on landing in fog in Rome; probably 30 Ugandans killed. We agree at Serote to be back around 1 o'clock. The first person we meet says he listens to the BBC and have we heard about the plane crash? Two Dutch women from the Médicins Sans Frontières (MSF) feeding centre pick us up by arrangement. We need a coffee after the early start and the 1-hour flight without breakfast. Serote was once a kind of up-country holiday rest town as well as a trading centre. There is a grid layout of some three streets crisscrossed by four. Cement-built shops are evident, some with ambitious pediments bearing a date and a name. The cool arcades give protection from the sun. Behind them there is a sizeable mosque.

Breakfast at the Uganda Coffee Shop – five waitresses in immaculate brown uniforms offer us coffee (what else?), then eggs and delicious hot rolls. My egg is almost crimson but does not taste too odd. 'They feed the chickens here on marijuana,' somebody says – does that account for the colour? It proves to be one of the better, unexpected breakfasts.

At the MSF feeding centre we see ginger-haired children with extended tummies, bulging eyes, matchstick legs and arms – the hallmarks of malnutrition. There are some 120 kids, accompanied by mothers and siblings. They get weak milk to start with, then fortified milk, then slowly build up if possible. The mothers are trained to do the cooking; others are responsible for hygiene. Each family group also lights its own fire and cooks. It's extraordinary to see 30 charcoal fires with 30 people bent low blowing up the charcoal to get heat. The tuberculosis ward has children of nine who look about five. The kids generally seize a passing adult hand as if for comfort. A woman sweeps the ground clean. The doctors try to keep up morale; they are calm and quiet. Catherine Bond questions an orphaned child; where and how were her parents lost? 'They were bewitched.' 'What does that mean?' 'They were bewitched.'

We go to the hospital next door, which has been much repaired by MSF. It has been newly painted and there are new roofs and clean wards. A Dutch doctor says there are 105 nurses out of a full complement of 150; and six doctors out of 15, but two of them are sick. They do get sterile supplies and drugs but in batches, and so they run out before they get the next batch. I see sealed drip-feed sets but a doctor says if they throw away the connector or needles they might still re-use the piping. There is a marvellous matron, immaculate in her white starched uniform, her tiny starched hat perched on coils of minutely plaited hair. In the women's surgical ward, one patient has had her leg broken and suffered a bad shrapnel wound from a helicopter attack. She claims four people were killed. In a nearby bed, there is a woman whose arm has been badly mauled by a hippo. They are one of the most dangerous beasts in the world, especially if you come between them and the water. The victim says she did not see the hippo in the long grass. Uganda is overgrown with neglect.

Outside the operating theatre, the white wellies are being scrubbed. One of the MSF people was shot in an 'ambush' – one of the great words of Serote – and received four bullets, two in the shoulder, one in the wrist and one in the stomach. The hospital removed two, staunched the bleeding and saved his life. In the male surgical ward, a man who was 'ambushed' has a leg wound; his four-year-old son was also shot. He works in Kampala for Cooper Cars, had returned to Serote to bring his family to Kampala and ended up ambushed. How unlucky can you get? We visit the District Administrator – he says things are better than six months ago; yes, some rebels have given up; yes, some rebels (or bandits) live in town by day and then go out to the countryside at night.

We set out to look at the no-man's land of neighbouring countryside towards Arupiya. On the main road, many people are walking back from market. We turn right at the Teso school. Grass stands head-high along the verges, and grows tall in the middle of the road. More than half the plots in the once cultivated fields are neglected and overgrown with grass. Some groups of thatched round huts – usually three or four – are deserted. Others contain a clutch of people. There is no livestock at all, only an extraordinary silence. We stop one man who says he nearly ran away because he thought we were soldiers who might beat him up. No one warns us not to go further.

After about 2 miles we are near the marsh and almost decide to turn back when we see a group of huts with people. There are five men, two of whom speak excellent English. They complain of the NRA soldiers: 'They come in, beat people up, ask "where are the rebels?"' The villagers deny they are rebels; they have no livestock; they cannot farm; their women occasionally buy 'greens' to eat. They bake clay pellets in the sun to put in their catapults to kill birds. Always it is the army of whom they complain. One shows faint scars on his arms where soldiers strung him up. Gradually people emerge from the surrounding fields. The women have been at a funeral nearby for a relative killed by troops recently – this corroborates the story of an older man we had met along the road half an hour earlier. In one of the huts they have a still where they make the local hooch – 'warigi' – a type of gin. There are two exquisitely fashioned earth and straw food stores, but they contain little food or grain.

The atmosphere is hot, abandoned, and threatened by nameless violence of an unpredictable kind (the 'bandits') or of an all too nameable kind, the supposedly 'better-disciplined' army. The bandits, if such they are, seem odd. Often they rob travellers of cameras. Next they will demand films. Finally, processing? By now it is very late, pushing 1 o'clock. We drive back, stop at the MSF doctors' home, thank them and go to the airport. As we approach we hear a plane climbing overhead. When we arrive the tarmac is bare – and nearby soldiers roar with laughter. I make gestures of farewell to the sky and mime demands that the plane should return. The soldiers laugh still more. We go to the army headquarters – can they get a helicopter or a plane up from Entebbe? A vain hope.

Back at the doctors' home, they feed us and mention that the Director of the Flying School lives next door. They also say that we were lucky not to have been 'ambushed' in the area we visited. Not long ago, a group of travellers was stopped by rebels, stripped naked and sent off back to Serote. Sitting safely in the doctors' house eating omelettes, the thought of Catherine Bond, George Bennett (Head of the BBC African Service) and myself returning from the bush without a stitch is only hysterical. Catherine Bond talks to the Director of the Flying School and he says by 2.30 we should have a plane. By 3 pm at the airfield, the Director, George

Oguli, is making mild efforts to get an instructing plane down to earth. The instructors appear to ignore him as they criss-cross the airfield. 'Are we going to get a plane?' we ask. The Director is re-assuring. By 4.30 the plane is down.

Before that we finally get through to Eileen Mullen in Kampala. She is desperate. We are certainly late. Have we crashed or been arrested? She will have to hold the news conference, then host the party until we arrive. But when will we arrive? The plane is being refuelled. Only after the instructor has finished debriefing his two pupils is it clear that he will not fly us on. However, a rather sharp Tanzanian instructor agrees to take us to Entebbe in return for his overnight costs. We finally set off at 5 pm.

It is a glorious flight, across green but neglected land and through dramatic cloud towers. We land at 5.50, find the car, and then get delayed by bad traffic. I reach the party at 7.15 and immediately launch into a speech. Various ministers are there: the Prime Minister, the Minister for Rehabilitation, the Foreign Minister, the head of the Government Inspectorate and the Head of the Human Rights Commission. The Russian Press attaché is also there with his sidekick from Tass. 'Hello, I am Igor. This is a great occasion. We are so glad to be invited. You know it is not a big party, but a very select one. Please, congratulations.' He has done his homework on me and insinuates references to our common Slavic origins. We get on to Albania – I say everyone should visit it in order to appreciate a fully functioning Stalinist dictatorship. 'You know,' replies Igor, 'five years ago we would reject such a provocation – today we agree with it.' I said we were so relaxed about things that the West would almost welcome a Soviet invasion of Romania. It has been a bizarre and extraordinary day.

TUESDAY 18 OCTOBER

A busy morning prior to flying out by Ethiopian Airlines to Lilongwe, then on to Harare. As I set out to see Katigaya, the Acting Prime Minister and close confidant of President Museveni, Eileen breaks the news – there is no Ethiopian Airlines flight. It stopped operating a few days ago. We cannot get to Harare that day. A tight schedule of meetings in Zimbabwe is threatened and a day of trauma begins.

Meanwhile I visit Katigaya, the Prime Minister. He is relaxed, safari-suited, direct. 'What is the government rehabilitation programme?' I ask. Firstly, they only look two years ahead. Secondly, they are concentrating on roads and transport, and on rehabilitating the Jinja power station. This will give Uganda most of the power it needs. Next, they plan a new dam further down the Nile. Then they need to reconstruct the people's attitude to work. A decade of destruction has undermined work and responsibility and endeavour. This is clearly a prerequisite. In the countryside they must build up livestock (now there are only three million animals, as against some 12 million previously). This will take years.

Why does President Moi of Kenya not get on with Museveni? The Ugandans are puzzled. Why not talk things over? they say. Katigaya suggests two possible reasons: Moi wanted an agreed settlement between Okello and Museveni; when the terms were put to the fighters they refused, so Museveni went on and won. Moi felt slighted; he also disliked the thought of anyone winning power in a guerrilla war (what an example?). Besides, Museveni is very casual and umpompous and very quick, it is said. Moi is more formal, even pompous, likes ceremony, is not a flexible thinker, and cannot get on with Museveni's style.

Back in the hotel, the future of the Zimbabwe trip is looking uncertain. Can we send a charter plane up from Nairobi? If so, how do we proceed from there? We take a decision and book a charter up from Nairobi the following morning. Alternatively, can the taxi firm drive us to Nairobi? After some thought, they say 'no'. They have the wrong insurance – and anyway it is a 12-hour drive. What about a High Commission car? The British drivers are hopeful and constructive. On the phone from Nairobi, Mike Wooldridge is very alarmed. Last time he drove through the Highlands at night, some gangs threw a boulder through the windscreen, all but killing two people. So we should stop at Eldoret around midnight, just short of the Highlands, then continue at dawn to catch the direct Kenyan Airways flight to Harare – but this is full. Ian Mills in Harare meanwhile suggests the flight to Lilongwe in Malawi, followed by a charter to Harare. But as this involves flying over rebel Renamo territory in Mozambique – where planes have been shot down with missiles – the Zimbabwean authorities will not contemplate this. By 4.30 it is clear that the High Commission car also lacks the necessary insurance, so another door closes.

To kill time we go to the Oxfam house overlooking Lake Victoria where the view of the lake and islands, reminiscent of Clew Bay in County Mayo in Ireland, is ravishing. There is much talk of the situation in the north, the minutiae of tribal movements, the impact of famine, the real state of malnutrition, and the difficulty of stirring up international enthusiasm to help relieve yet another famine. Oxfam says it is spending too much of its time on emergency relief, too little on real development. Of over 100 development schemes in nominal existence, most have not been visited or checked on in years. Another topic of conversation is an account of Sudanese game park wardens who were incensed by wildlife poaching from Uganda. They crossed the border, found the suspects, tortured them until they sang, shot some and gave the others a 'proper beating' (usually defined as stopping just short of death).

Over dinner at the hotel we consider the increasingly crazy options. Ian Mills now suggests a flight from Nairobi to Lusaka, followed by a drive to the border and changing to another car in Zimbabwe. I say I will not fly anywhere on the off-chance of being able to move on. Wooldridge counters with the Swissair flight from Nairobi to Johannesburg early, followed by Kenyan Airways to Harare. This depends on us being early on our single-engined charter or Swissair being untypically late. Advice fluctuates: it is worth going; it is not worth going. I am strongly tempted to cancel, especially as my stomach is not quite right, but I am also reluctant to run out on the trip. The only sure thing is that the charter will be ready to leave by 9 am. We decide to set out early to get a flying start and with luck make the Swissair flight (if it is delayed).

WEDNESDAY 19 OCTOBER

Another dawn over Kampala, with the kites wheeling in swarms around the hotel and the white egrets and hooded crows in great groups. The egrets crowd the trees like Christmas decorations as they queue to drink at the ornamental fountains. We leave at 7.30 with Samuel, our trusty driver. All goes well until the first NRA post. It is clear they have decided to take an interest in money.

One teenage youth riffles through my travellers' cheques and currency form. I have quite a number, so reconciling them would be a difficult task for a good bank clerk, never mind a semi-literate soldier. He does not attempt to count or to reconcile. He appears satisfied and gives it all back to me.

Eileen Mullen gets a far tougher going-over from another youth. It gets worse when a young officer joins in. He believes he knows. And things look black when he holds $7500 travellers' cheques, and says they have not been declared, so they will be confiscated. Very patiently Eileen explains the difference between pounds and dollars, and the fact that we have Ugandan shillings which we need to change back. She stays very calm, very unflustered, and finally the officer agrees that all is in order.

Then they get to George Bennett. We know that he is $360 short because he was not given a foreign currency receipt for the Serote charter. This will look bad – as if we have traded on the black market. But George is brilliant. He is deliberately very slow: constantly taking things back to check them; constantly pulling out something else as if that was the answer. His masterstroke is to produce his Seychelles rupees. This seems to blow them altogether and they give up without spotting the missing dollars.

Then the officer turns to me and says 'Now you'. I say I have already been done. He looks doubtful, I point to a young soldier, he shrugs and after 25 very long minutes we drive on. Samuel, incidentally, had to open the boot as well. They were undoubtedly looking for the chance to steal some money. Our unwitting tactic of patience, firmness and refusal to give any money as a bribe paid off. Desmond Morris saved us; like animals, we kept a low physical profile, avoiding too much eye contact.

We are then stopped at the airport NRA post. They look through bags and handbags, but in a comparatively cursory way. We are late. Changing our shillings back takes time and much form-filling. Then there is customs; then the aircraft manifest. We wait on the tarmac for Steve, the pilot, for 20 minutes and leave around 10 am (an hour late) in a Cessna Centurion, one-engined, high-winged plane.

It is a glorious flight, though we all spend our time wondering what to do if we ditch in Lake Victoria. How far can we swim? Is there a clear strip of land on that island if we crash-land? Lake

Victoria is vast, broad and magnificently island-strewn. Over North Kenya the land is undulating, green and well cultivated. Then we are into cattle land. It is more arid, and the circular kraals for cattle surrounded by round straw huts look like diagrams from a natural geography book. The soil gets black, almost volcanic. Then the edge of the Rift valley shows ahead. There is a steep drop into the parched valley bottom. And we see a huge extinct volcano with a jagged mouth and harsh runnels of old lava and watercourses scarring its sides. Nairobi lies on the opposite lip of the rift. Its masses of purple jacaranda look even more extraordinary from the air. We buck our way into Jomo Kenyatta Airport to be told that the Swissair flight has gone. I learn, too, that three of our African Service producers on a publicity trip up-country have been arrested. But that is another story.

At the end of three weeks in Kenya, Uganda and Zimbabwe, one Zimbabwean journalist consoles me that the attention devoted to us at official political levels is often critical. 'Whatever Heads of State say about you, be under no illusion, they all listen.' The BBC draws attention for good and ill. It is a very responsible position to hold and the responsibility of our journalism must match it. I have learned that governments and politicians play it rough; and when threatened they play it very rough indeed. Journalism in Africa is a tender plant. TV and radio are rudimentary, the press crude and intermittently professional. The gap between what governments can – and should – do for their people is huge. I sense a continent slipping back, not keeping up with the existing challenge. In Kenya, the feudal atmosphere deriving from the total power of the President leads subordinates to act in a way they believe the 'king' would approve of – if he approves, then that is the law. We cannot be intimidated by such actions, or by the difficulty of doing things in Africa. Not all of Africa is like Uganda – far from it. But in the sense that Uganda still has a very long way to go, so does Africa. In Africa, always something difficult. Or as one old hand commented: 'Africa always wins.'

'WE HAVE LOST THE
ELECTION'

POLAND, 1–6 JUNE 1989

THURSDAY 1 JUNE

Warsaw airport is a perfect introduction to the country – the trivial is the microcosmic image of the whole. Here they are short of facilities: just two baggage carousels for the whole international airport; no signs telling you which plane is being unloaded where; too few people at immigration and customs. The system is like Moscow but one-tenth as efficient – or relentless – and no longer carried out with conviction. At some airports you can smell fear and police on arrival; there is no such smell here. There are hordes of people, crowding into the arrivals hall and on to the waving balcony, a sign of a Third World economy, and one where people still travel comparatively little. Journeys, and departing or visiting relatives, are therefore a major ritual and are treated with appropriate seriousness. In London, the only people who wait for you are hired drivers and limo cars; such is the decline of conviviality.

The air is hot and humid as Karol Malcuzynski, the BBC office manager, drives me to the Victoria Intercontinental. He has worked out a good list of meetings including ones with Rakowski, Glemp and Walesa. We go for a quick walk through the nearby park with the War Memorial. Polish schoolchildren openly snigger at the eternally ridiculous goose-stepping changing of the guard. But the names on the memorial are a plangent reminder of the closeness of Anglo-Polish wartime co-operation: Narvik, Arnhem, Monte Cassino, some of the great failures of the war.

FRIDAY 2 JUNE

A damp and muggy day. Warsaw is looking very grey and dreary. Off to Janusz Onyskiewicz's office, a smallish flat in a grey slab block. But the corridors are clean, the stairwells do not smell, and there is no reek of poverty. Onyskiewicz arrives five minutes late after an overnight train journey from his constituency. He is shortish and cheerful, apologises for being unshaven, and goes off to get rid of the stubble. He talks very directly and seems amazingly relaxed after the weeks of campaigning. Going up in the lift he says the main problem for Solidarnosc may be not to do too well. What does he mean by that? Well, if there are too many voters who deliberately strike out the National List – the government list – as an act of revenge, if Solidarnosc sweeps the Senate and the 35 per cent of the open seats, and if many senior officials are struck out and fail to get their 50 per cent, then the government and the Party will be demoralised. Onyskiewicz says that the Soviet Union did not give 'permission' for the Round Table compromise; if they had a role it was to indicate that so long as alliances and foreign policy were maintained, communication with East Germany kept open, and so long as the Party retained its leading role, then the Poles could do what they wanted especially if it guaranteed stability.

At the BBC office, the new correspondent, Kevin Connolly, leads me to lunch at the Actors Club, with its wonderful faded ancient decor, redolent of old Central Europe. But who are the people? Not as many actors as there used to be; the Polish intellectuals are heavily interlarded with diplomats and correspondents. I came here 15 years ago and it has hardly changed. The service is spectacularly slow but the duck is first class – full of flavour, and generous in its fat content though the meat is plentiful too. We pick up Andrew Taussig (Controller of European Services) who was lucky not to be diverted on his flight from Vienna because of one of the heavy thunderstorms that fill our days in Warsaw.

From there we move on to the offices of the new official Solidarnosc daily *Gazetta Wyborcza* (*Election Gazette*), which is printed on official government presses. They say circulation is half a million for the weekly, with a readership of two million for the daily. The offices are in a disused kindergarten in a Warsaw suburb, condemned on health grounds, though evidently good enough for journalists. We talk to a Deputy Editor, Krzystof Sliwinski, a distinguished Catholic intellectual. His fears are of a lot of confusion in the voting; the lists are so complicated; they will take too long to fill in; will the polls get overcrowded? Should voters vote early? He rates Archbishop Glemp highly and says he was Cardinal Wyszinski's choice. As he lay dying, he was phoned by Wojtyla, the 'Pope from Poland', who had been shot and nearly killed by Ali Agca some four days earlier. Glemp was passed on to the Pope as the designated successor. Not an intellectual; not an orator; but a decent man. And a man who knows his duty – if it is to be martyred for his faith, then martyred he would be. He is, in his own terms, and often described by others as, a decent honourable man.

Sliwinski agrees that the Catholic Party is growing in strength and implies it has a political role to play. A *Gazetta* columnist joins us and says the economic outlook is bleak. Political reform is one thing; but there will then be a difficult transition once economic reform tries to catch up with political reform. The intervening period will be difficult. They agree that the gap between Solidarnosc as a party and Solidarnosc as a union can only become more problematic as time goes by and compromises have to be made. The *Gazetta* is largely staffed by former underground journalists. They work on brand-new word processors, each former kindergarten room clearly labelled as editorially responsible for a different page or column. There is an air of quiet professionalism. How extraordinary that with this handful of people they can get a half-million circulation – the miracles of desktop publishing.

Dinner at the Victoria Hotel with Daniel Passant, Deputy Editor of *Politika*, and Krzystof Woyna, commentator on Polish radio and TV. They are candid about the Party's failings. It is normal, they say, that candidates should stand in their own right and their own name, not in that of the Communist Party. The unstated belief is that the Communist Party cannot credibly run on the strength of any kind of appeal to its past record, so the individual achievement or personality of the candidate is what counts. It is an incredible turnaround. We had all heard, or watched, Jaruzelski's TV speech beforehand. He made no appeal for support from the Communist Party – he only mentioned the Party once. He did appeal for a coalition after the election – the Party will guarantee stability and reform – an appeal of a sort, but essentially a weak last-ditch one. It is extraordinary to find the Communist Party being treated as an irrelevance, yet no one, not even these two 'official' journalists, makes any attempt to defend or even set out a Party line, except that of reform. But why trust the Party to reform the hideous demeaning mess which it has spent the last 40 years creating?

Our dinner is mildly disrupted by a solo American/Franco/Pole at the next table who is a Mr Knowall. His helpful advice on Balkan Cabernet ('excellent'), smoked duck ('more strong than in Western Europe') and politics ('I've been to Auschwitz – let me tell you, never forget history; it could happen again') make him a Grade A bore. We slough him off before long.

Overall the political atmosphere could not be more extraordinary. It is relaxed, open, confident but not euphoric. What is different is that the Russians are absent. Their views are no longer felt to be important.

SATURDAY 3 JUNE

Off to see Archbishop Glemp. The Archepiscopal Palace is grand, extensive and well kept. Inside the entrance, the air is heavy with polish and an effortlessly managed calm that comes only from high authority. A very tall young priest secretary with a green sash around his waist listens to Karol's announcement of our appointment and shows us into the waiting room. Actually, with a throne at one end, a picture of Wojtyla over the throne and a series of official portraits of Glemp's predecessors, it is really the audience room. It has a polished floor, immaculate decor, and a calming view of the palace grounds.

It comes as a surprise when the door behind us opens and Glemp strides in without any fuss or fanfare. He is like his pictures: short, with a comfortable pot belly, smooth skin, large ears, direct brown eyes, and looking younger than his reputed 60 years. He has a quiet voice and gives direct simple answers; not subtle or obviously clever but thoughtful and sensitive. He regards Marxism-Leninism as finished, existing only as a habit of thought and behaviour out of which the people must be educated, though he clearly does not see this as a speedy process. The resorting to collective action rather than assuming individual responsibility is perceived as a moral, philosophical problem. He agrees that the Soviet Union has not been an active partner in sharing recent events in Poland; but its withdrawal as a participant-adviser has been crucial. Glemp sees difficulties for Solidarnosc as a trade union and as a political party. He believes that the Catholic Party will grow and we sense that he would like to see it do so. He concedes that Solidarnosc has a special part in the Church's heart, but he disapproves of its attempt to be the sole participant in power with the Communist Party. There is a kind of monopolism that he does not like and that produces a very direct whiff of disapproval.

As we leave, Karol asks him if he thinks Glemp's brother – a Communist Party candidate – will do well. The Archbishop laughs and says the whole thing has been dreamed up to discredit him. On the Jewish protest against the nuns at Auschwitz he says the convent is a long-standing one, and the walls are outside the camp. Anyway, there ought to be prayer at such a place – he hints that the very concept of a place too damned to pray in is alien to Christianity – and he fears that the Zionist protest may produce a backlash of anti-Semitism. The green-sashed priest bows us out elegantly.

Karol drives us to Gdansk, through rain, lightning and roads deep in water, silver and curving like rivers. We find only three filling stations en route. In Poland most filling stations have queues, and some have petrol. The trick is to find the latter without the former. One has a long queue. The second is OK and has petrol. Karol puts on his Korean-made fuzz-buster, an anti-police radar device. It emits high shrieks when it finds a radar beam. He brakes sharply, slows down to a walk and cruises past the parked police car waving cheerfully. He shows us the curve where the secret police first tried to kill Father Popieluszko, with a brick through his windscreen, to be followed by an accidental fire in the ruins of the crashed car. Then the layby where the police left their car and signalled his appearance in advance to the brick throwers. But Popieluszko's driver was quick-witted. He drove at the police, rather than swerving away, and put them off their aim. So the priest survived one attack. The land is open, fertile, unspoiled and slightly built up, though well cultivated. This is horse-drawn vehicle land, with the occasional family group hoeing in the fields. It is rolling, gentle, remote and a generation away from intensive cultivation.

The Hotel Hevelius in Gdansk has the special anomie of large hotels in provincial towns – the Sheraton in Kampala is one, the Belfast Europa is another. You sense boredom as you come in through the doors. I go out to see the Gdansk Shipyard Memorial which is easily visible from my hotel windows. As I photograph the entrance of the shipyard, an old gatekeeper beckons me over with a disapproving wave. He speaks in Polish. I gesture incomprehension. German? Yes. It is forbidden to photograph. I express regret as an ordinary tourist. He nods. Where am I from? His brother works in Manchester. Then the cruncher: 'Mein lieber Freund, haben Sie Dollars?' I explain that, incredibly, I have none. He sighs sadly, and tells me he saw the 1960 strikes when workers were shot down on this very spot. I go off to the memorial 50 yards away. There are women, children, flowers, banners and hurrying camera crews. Then a small group of people – not including Walesa – appear, lay flowers and make a solemn speech. It is not grand but it is moving. The crowd dissolves. As I move away I see that the mound on which the memorial stands is deserted except for two women, ordinary, in their aprons. Their hands are raised in the Solidarnosc salute; no one there to see them.

Karol Malcuzynski, Andrew Taussig and I take a taxi to Lech Walesa's house for his name day party. He lives in a solid two-storey house on the edge of Gdansk, in a leafy road. There is a good size garden or rather small orchard. It is not palatial and not huge for his family of eight but a cut above his former flat. And why not? How many electricians have undermined a Communist state? There are already camera crews at the party. We push through, present him with a bottle of whisky, congratulate him on his name day and are invited to tuck in. Mrs Walesa – small, pretty, delicate-featured and very relaxedly cheerful – says, 'I don't want to hear elections or politics discussed' (a vain hope). Lech is large, broad-shouldered, now stout, wearing a slightly rumpled version of the clichéd cotton Italian-style checked suit. He has a light voice, quick eyes, and a sharp manner. He may have slowed down a little but his voice still moves nimbly. Above all he seems to wear his relentless exposure to public attention easily. He is 'Lech' to everyone; he is owned; he belongs; he seems to accept that burden.

There is a stir. Important guests have arrived – Mrs Barbara Johnson, the widowed Polish-American millionairess who has declared she will take over the Gdansk shipyards. She is of medium height, slightly broad-featured, with heavily peroxided hair and a poor, light complexion. She wears a perpetual but rather vacant smile. She does not look rich as American women usually do but like the very rich she is surrounded and protected. Ahead of her – sleek, silky and possessive – comes Father Jankowski, the priest of St Brygidda's, the 'Solidarnosc Church'. His benign calculating smile takes in everyone. The greetings from Lech are fulsome. But it is the Johnson entourage who demand attention. Two representatives from the Polish National Congress of America, well aware that their presence at this rescue mission for the birthplace of Solidarity will raise their standing in every chapter of that large and influential body. Then three Johnson lawyers, not so much taking part in the celebrations as watching them, as if their client's interests might need their professional protection even on such an occasion. They remind me of Ping, Pang and Pong from *Turandot*, observers and commentators, flitting somewhat restlessly from room to room as if every movement might turn into a deal which they should monitor. I almost expect to be charged for a few moment's party gossip. They are not good for the party atmosphere, which the Irish television team certainly are.

As I come in I notice a man with a dog collar shooting on a 16mm Arriflex camera. Am I seeing right? I ask a young man with a sound recorder across his shoulder. Yes, the priest is a freelance film-maker who sells documentaries to RTE. He is both a practising priest and a working documentary film-maker – a television worker priest, you might say. All three of the crew are charming. Their translator is more eccentric. He floats around the party for some long time until we come face to face. First he talks of Conrad, the Pole who ended up writing the most immaculate, precise English. Then he moves on to Nijinsky. Did I know that he too was Polish, known to Poles as 'Nas Nijinsky' ('Our Nijinsky')? Did I know it was his centenary? Did I know that the world's greatest living expert on Nijinsky lived in Warsaw and couldn't I find time to see him? Would I make sure that the World Service did some programmes on Nijinsky? I murmur some objection about ballet not working well on radio and move away.

After the first flurry associated with the arrival of the Johnson party, suddenly there is another cry – 'Lech, Lech come out'. The car cavalcade which I saw starting up in a modest way in the middle of town earlier has arrived. Ordinary cars, beaten-up Polonezs, Fiat 500s, old cars, cars filled with families, covered with Solidarnosc posters, trailing Solidarnosc flags, waving the two-finger salute, and beating their horns in the 'pah-pah-pahpahpah' salute. Walesa and Barbara Johnson come out to the road verge and stand surrounded by a crowd of over a hundred acknowledging the cheers. Some cars stop and the driver rushes out either to embrace Lech, to give him flowers or to get his auto-graph. Lech's driver, the bodyguard and organiser, waves them on furiously. On more than one occasion, the crowd breaks into the Polish birthday song 'Sto Lat' ('a hundred years'). From the window of a military hospital opposite, a nurse leans out from a barred window and makes the Solidarnosc sign. The cars turn round and come back on the other side of the road. It takes 45 minutes before they have had enough. The spontaneous emotion poured out is quite extraordinary. This is real politics.

We return to the house. Then Lech is dragged out to the back yard to do an interview with Polish TV for the eve of the poll main news bulletin. He is calm and cheerful, and makes one essential point. He will vote for the National List – ruling out only one person (undoubedly the leader of the 'official' trade union, Myodorowicz) – but urging Solidarnosc supporters to do the same. Lech's mood is conciliatory, echoing that of Jaruzelski on TV the previous evening and confirming the view that Solidar-nosc is anxious about the scale of the victory. Within 20 minutes everyone clusters around the TV set in the Walesa drawing room to watch his (uncut) interview transmitted. (In Warsaw two days later we hear from Geremek and others that the Solidarnosc headquarters received scores of phone calls demanding to know why Lech said 'Vote for the National List'. John Lloyd of the *Financial Times* tells me that in a tour of several Solidarnosc offices between Warsaw and Gdansk not a single committee intended to do anything but cross out the entire National List.) Mrs Walesa insists we have soup and chicken before we go. The food is fresh and excellent. We thank Lech, wish him well on his name day once more, and return to the gloomy, echoing Hotel Hevelius.

SUNDAY 4 JUNE

Today takes off where the previous day ended. I have an hour walking round the Old Town, a typical Hanseatic League city: rich merchants' houses, elaborately stepped gables, elevated terraces at the front of the houses, the steps flanked with carved statues or figures, redolent of mercantile wealth. The streets are broad, there are thick city walls, a large town square and several vast churches. It's a slice of medieval life still intact. Also stuck in amber are the silver and amber shops; the whole street reeks of the German tourist trade.

We are a bit late for Mass at St Brygidda's. The crowd spills out of the doors and listens to the broadcast outside. Karol takes us in through the vestry. Lech's driver beckons us to go and sit down. We are in the choir, seated by Father Jankowski, in the row in front of Lech and some of his family. Another priest is officiating. Lo and behold it is the Irish film director, clad in resplendent Polish robes. The crowd is densely packed. Then rich voices and a smoothly sung service which totally ignores – or accepts – the cameramen flitting around Lech and his family. Father Jankowski moves up to the lectern to deliver the homily. He begins in a mat-ter-of-fact tone of voice until I suddenly realise he is welcoming the 'BBC from London'. There is a long burst of applause. I catch Lech's eye. He grins broadly and nods. Jankowski talks for some 20 minutes, about the concept of homeland and responsibility, he tells me later. He is a passionate speaker, and draws three bursts of applause. He does not sound like a rabble-rouser. Jankowski has his detractors but there is no denying the man's authority.

Then the Mass. For me it can never replace the Anglican Com-munion text, and I cannot overlook communion in one kind only. But I accept the wafer – it would be churlish not to – and reflect on the extraordinary contrast with Communion at St George's, Windsor, only two weeks ago. Both, for their own congregations, are true acts of devotion. As the Irish television priest returns from delivering the Host through the packed crowds, Jankowski launches into an incredibly florid 'Ite Missa Est', like an operatic tenor lamenting the end of a great event. There is one moment of pure surrealism from a Buñuel film. Towards the end of the Mass, a figure materialises by my side. It is 'Nijinsky'. He tugs my sleeve. The world's greatest expert on Nijinsky will see me in Warsaw –

can I arrange a time? I do not believe this is happening. I snap at him that I have no time and he subsides.

Karol ushers us to the priest's house courtyard as the gates are opened and the crowd floods in for the speeches. Camera crews are parked on the monument to the Virgin in the middle of the yard. Boys climb on to the walls to get a better view. A microphone wire is lowered from an upper storey window; Lech's driver tests it to satisfaction. Then Jankowski, Lech and the American National Congress brigade start the serious business.

It is mainly about the shipyard. One of the lawyers told RTE that he would do an interview, provided they did not ask about lay-offs. Yet here is Mrs Johnson, asked directly by Jankowski if they will take back the 6000 or so workers laid off, and she says 'Yes'. No wonder they cheer, sing 'Sto Lat' again, and look happy. Lech says the agreement – only in outline – has taken a burden off his mind. The air is heavy with hopes raised, only to be dashed in the future. There is an understandable wish to believe that all will be well.

Finally, the crowds disperse. The priest's house is large. There are photos of Jankowski with the Pope. Paintings of the same, the son bending his head before the loving father, cover the entrance walls. The sitting room has a large bureau cupboard carved out of thick black wood. Paintings of cardinals and a severe-looking Pilsudski cover the walls here. There is much to-ing and fro-ing. The Irish priest/TV producer says he doesn't like the Pope, but adds inconsequentially that he does like Cardinal O'Fiaigh. We are ushered into the priest's dining room where there is more heavily carved furniture in black. A long table set for 20 people is covered with lace tablecloths, and flags of Poland, America, France and Britain are dotted along its length. There are silver knives and forks resting on silver supports, and three glasses each, including one, deep-cut and coloured. This is the dining room where over the years Solidarnosc's fortunes have been planned and saved and defended. Here Mrs Thatcher spoke for three hours with Lech. I ask Mrs Johnson about her plans. When did she decide to buy the shipyard? On Corpus Christi in a procession with Lech. Isn't it a risk? No, the people are right and it is people who count. (But how many people will you count?) She sees no risk; look at their experience in Sczeczin. No, she feels unusually confident about it.

Jankowski comes over as confident but not overly so; very much in command, and direct without over-elaboration. Is he a political priest? No, he does only those things to serve the community that the Church sees as its duty. In his homily he spoke of citizenship and responsibility, a theme that will be increasingly relevant as the years go by. Has his bishop disapproved? Not the present one. The former bishop, under heavy police pressure, suggested a move. Jankowski declined. The police came and suggested that at least a holiday abroad would be a good idea. Jankowski was at this stage refusing to encourage the workers to end their post-martial law sit-in. So he went abroad with a family of three in a new Mercedes given him by a German bishop for the purpose of distributing the food parcels and gifts flooding in. They arrived in West Germany. A few minutes after dropping Jankowski at the hotel, the family of three were killed when the steering broke. A coincidence, or a murder attempt on him?

What did I think of the Church service? Marvellous and impressive. He looks pleased. He praises the BBC Polish Service, saying it is fair and balanced and does not have the bias of Radio Free Europe and Voice of America. This point is made equally firmly by Walesa. Jankowski says he would like to start his own radio station. If so, I say he should get a satellite dish from Mrs Johnson and then rebroadcast the Polish Section. Walesa complains mildly to Andrew Taussig that we give too much attention to small, unrepresentative groups. Andrew replies that that is just what the government has said about Solidarnosc all these years. He takes the point. It's so easy to change from poacher to gamekeeper. Walesa tells Andrew that he thinks Jaruzelski and Rakowski are very isolated and lost. He thinks they want to be included in his family, so to speak, to lay their heads on his shoulder and to be loved. It is a shrewd observation.

We take the final photos, say farewell, thank the team of four ladies, two men and two boys who made the lunch of duck, pork and meat rissole, and return to Warsaw. It is a fast, dry drive at first. We hear the World Service 1300 *News* and *24 Hours* – brilliant coverage of Beijing and the Ayatollah's death. They made the bulletin an illustrated one with correspondents' despatches, quite rightly. We complete our journey through pouring rain and go to an Old Town restaurant for dinner. One tragedy – it is polling day and there is no vodka.

MONDAY 5 JUNE

Will the poll results start to show a definite trend? I have my first meeting with Jerzy Urban, Chairman of TV and Radio. He is small and round, with huge ears. Pudgy, wary and calculating, he holds your gaze steadily as he talks. He is dismissive of his opponent – 'a mere actor'. He had declined to debate with Urban, the fact he, Urban, was obliged to point out. What, after all, could the actor have said to questions about reform of income tax? It was time for Solidarnosc to shoulder responsibility. They couldn't endlessly oppose. The election was a trap to draw them into the responsibility they had avoided and they had fallen into it (sic). No, the Soviets were not involved in the Round Table decision and the decision to press for reform. The government were the reformers, Solidarnosc were hooked on their mass base. Yes, they did read *Pravda* but there had been nothing about events in Poland. Western commentators exaggerated the role of the USSR. The Polish democratic model was not like the Western one. That was founded on a solid base of democratic institutions and associations which did not exist in Poland. They still had to be created. Urban smokes two pipes, drawing evil, sweet-smelling tobacco from a capacious soft leather bag. At least he has the decency to open the window when he lights up. He is hard to penetrate. (Even then Urban must have known that the reviled actor was defeating him. He even lost the vote among Poles who voted in Moscow.)

I get back to the BBC office where the first results are heavily in favour of Solidarnosc and the picture is looking gloomy for the government. Karol says he has got Ciosek, a Politburo member to see us at 12, just before a leading government Round Table adviser, Reykowski (an academic like Solidarnosc's Geremek).

Off to the Central Committee building – the physical corridors of power: longer, with taller doors, a better finish, larger offices, and an atmosphere that is somehow less intimidating than it should be. In the offices of Ciosek's assistant, there are brand-new volumes of Lenin, some still in their cardboard cases, evidently untouched by human hand. We are ushered into the big Ciosek office. He comes in quickly – a large man, balding, stomach bulging a bit over his waistband, sweating. He is in a hurry. 'I had not had an appointment for you in my diary but I thought I should see you to let you know what is happening.' It is shortly after midday. We have not had a chance to open our mouths or put a question. But it is quite unnecessary.

'We are losing the election. We took the risk and I am one of those who decided we should take the risk. The architects of reform will not be elected to parliament.' I reach over for Karol's notebook and start writing. 'The defeat of the National List is a violation of the Round Table agreement but we have to live with it. We must now exist with a strong opposition. The governing coalition will have to live with less than 60 per cent of the seats in the Sejm. It is possible that the whole National List will perish.' We sit there open-mouthed at this incredible admission of electoral defeat by a Communist leader.

He continues: 'The whole opposition apparatus compaigned on an appeal to oppose the National List. Walesa's appeal was too late. Their attack was concentrated on the 8 per cent who made up the National List.' The extraordinary thing is that Ciosek is not violent, not resentful, just as hyped up as someone who has emerged from a crisis meeting – still continuing – would be. If it is a violation of the Round Table, I ask, are they repudiating it? 'No – an agreement is an agreement – now it is the will of the nation. But maybe the Round Table agreement should be amended to take account of the violation.' He seizes a piece of paper and sketches out the exact nature of the political deadlock. The Upper House is 100 per cent Solidarnosc. The Lower House, as a result of the destruction of the National List, is only 57 per cent for the government. Hence, they lack the two-thirds majority needed to override a Senate veto. 'The paralysis of the National Assembly is both a theoretical and a practical possibility.' We press him. What next?

'They have not yet discussed a coalition but that could be the way out.' He warms to his theme. 'The opposition has a moral obligation to co-operate.' I ask if they had foreseen these results in some way beforehand. He agrees that Jaruzelski's offer of a coalition was in part a response to the feared result. But the clear implication was that no one had thought it would be this bad. We discuss the various possibilities. Ciosek warns that Solidarnosc cannot manage things by themselves. They may in any case become divided and will not be able to remain united. 'If Solidarnosc took over the government and did not get $20 billion foreign aid immediately, they would soon lose their popularity. Economic sacrifices are the first problem. Either there are to be restrained living standards or the West will give us big sacks of money. The latter is not likely.' Then, with emphasis, 'We will form a coalition to lead us out of crisis.' And then his final thoughts (it is past 12.30 and I can feel the seconds ticking away to Kevin Connolly's next deadline): 'Neither the government nor the opposition have the ability to force the people to accept sacrifices.' He needs to get back to his crisis meeting – and I need to get to the phone. I dictate the main points to Kevin, he files for the 1300 *Newsreel* and it leads the Polish story and other competitors for some 6 hours.

We reel upstairs to a smaller office occupied by Mr Rekowski, a university academic who carried out the small Round Table talks – the detailed ones – with his academic opposite number, Geremek. Being an academic, he is more cautious about the figures but this is only habit. He must know the game is up. Not a dislikable man, he talks of the next negotiations with Geremek and the situation in which Poland now finds itself. He warns, without appearing to threaten, of the dangers of the anti-reformists. Poland has no tradition of active democracy. Alternation of power was not part of the Round Table agreement. Given the uncertainties, and the failure of the Round Table strategy – as seen by the government – there are some who might want it overturned. He speaks of Poland being like Spain before Franco. Once he even speaks of the 'Chinese solution'. It is bizarre to hear that idea raised as a solution to anything except to the ending of several thousand people's lives. In general he appears to be at a loss, understandably, as to what to do next.

Our next stop is Solidarnosc Headquarters to drag Geremek out for lunch. He is already giving two interviews against a marvellous wall of election posters. Every Solidarnosc candidate is pictured with Lech – the symbol of Poland. As he finishes, Karol seizes him, puts him into the car and drives round the park to what would be a very smart parkside eatery anywhere else but Poland. It is nice by Polish standards – but they are tragically low. Geremek is bearded and grizzled. He speaks simply, preferring

French to heavily accented English, but his French is more than good enough.

Over a hurried borscht, coke, and veal escalope, Geremek is economical and to the point. What should Solidarnosc do in this extraordinary situation? He is strongly opposed to being lured into a coalition, where the Communist Party has the power and Solidarnosc provides the moral authority. In any case, the government ministries are not the real seats of power. If there is a transfer of power, then you cannot overlook the 1.5 million posts of the 'Nomenklatura', whose members really represent the Communist Party at all levels. Without a clean-out there, talk of transfer of power is meaningless. Geremek specialises in medieval history. He plots current politics with all the authority and instinct of someone who has been in it for a lifetime.

Back at Solidarnosc Headquarters, the journalists are spilling out on to the pavement because the room in which Geremek and others are holding a press conference is already jammed. Cameramen are trying to get a shot through the barred windows. Everyone knows the world is turning over.

That evening, I run into Mark Frankland of *The Observer*. 'What I cannot get over', he says, 'is that after 40 years of Communist rule, they have created a political scene where they are the only people who can rule this country. Everyone else has been excluded from the political process for over a generation. How can they be expected to run the country, never mind clear up the Communist mess?'

Warsaw is quiet. No rejoicing, no massive police presence. No arguing with facts. Reality has broken in.

'IF THEY SPOKE
WITH ONE VOICE . . .'

PAKISTAN, 6–25 AUGUST 1989

8 AUGUST

There are two topics of conversation in post-Zia, Benazir Pakistan. Will Benazir stop rowing with the opposition, or are both sides stuck in their compulsive bickering? And, are the Afghan Mujaheddin worth supporting militarily, given that no one outside the government and the US Embassy appears to believe in a military solution in Afghanistan? One of post-Zia Pakistan's pleasures is the press – open, critical, well written, trenchant. Breakfast on the Embassy Residence terrace overlooking the Marghalla Hills is enlivened by three good newspapers: *The Muslim*, *The Nation* and *The Pakistan Times*. Each seems to take it in turns to criticise the Afghan Interim Government and its impotence and factionalism.

Phil Jones, the BBC stringer, takes me to see the United Nations Special Representative, Bennon Savan. He shuttles in and out of Kabul offering the UN's 'good offices', a thankless task. His opening comment is: 'Najib is winning by not losing; the Mujaheddin are losing by not winning.' Najib has several things on his side: he is an Afghan; he has an organisation; he has a chain of command; and the Mujaheddin have none of these things. Najib and the Russians are now turning back on the Mujaheddin the proposals they used to make on elections for example. 'Let us have elections. They say they will be rigged. All right, send in whomever you want to supervise them.' Najib realises that the Mujaheddin – split some 15 ways between the seven external groups and the eight internal fighters – would simply fragment in an election.

Savan is used to being abused by the Afghan Foreign Minister, Wakil: 'The last time I was there he shouted at me for 80 minutes, about how awful the UN was. When he stopped, I was silent. "Don't you have anything to say?" he asked. "Yes, I'm going to send you a goddam bill. You can talk like that to your mother but not to me. I don't have to take that stuff ". Then he calmed down.' Savan believes the military option is non-existent, and the only answer is a political one. But the Benazir government doesn't seem to have any in mind. Savan is a largeish Armenian Cypriot with a rich, slightly fractured vocabulary and the invaluable instinct of the bargainer. He is a cabaret turn but now his punchline is: 'OK fire me; I don't want to stay; you can all go to hell.' From his experience in Kabul the Mujaheddin rockets have tended to land on civilian targets. 'They say they're landing on the Soviet Embassy. Well it's the fastest rebuilt embassy compound that I've ever seen.'

Why should anybody in Kabul risk defecting to the Mujaheddin, asks Savan. Most of them assume that a fundamentalist government would exact a dreadful revenge; 'If you're an ordinary Kabul shopkeeper, what do you think your chances will be of explaining to an Islamic court that you didn't collaborate? Too risky, so stick to Najib.'

Later, I call on the Pakistani Foreign Minister, Yaqub Khan, a splendid figure in white: fine, sharp features, grey hair swept back to reveal an imposing forehead, long white high-collared coat, white trousers, white ankle-length boots made of leather plaits and zipped up the side, half an inch of marcella shirt cuff showing, with a gold cufflink sporting a deep blue stone, gold chain holding gold pince-nez and a gold chain across his waist. He puts a very revealing rhetorical question in answer to one about Afghanistan. 'Why is it that a year ago, the Afghan Army was deserting, the civil service couldn't be trusted, the Red Army was being defeated, Najib was a Soviet puppet, the Mujaheddin were the Davids of the struggle, the UN was behind them, they commanded the attention and admiration of the whole world, the Soviet Union was attacked for its involvement? Now, a year later, the Soviet Union has won the kudos for withdrawal, Najib looks like a nationalist leader, his army is not deserting but fighting and winning, the Kabul regime has some public strength, and the Mujaheddin are divided, not believed, losing support and sympathy, and are suddenly looking like an unattractive, disorganised, unworthy body of fighters? Why is it?' Well, he does not stay for an answer but he does not need to. His posing of the question in those terms is its own answer.

Western and Pakistani journalists are at one in their analysis of the military naïvety and political impotence of the Afghan Interim Government. No one can account for the policy vacuum on this issue in the Benazir government, unless it is fear of a fundamentalist outcry by the Opposition.

11 AUGUST

To Peshawar, the seat of the Interim Government, gateway to Afghanistan, the gun-runners, black marketeers and drug barons. One half is the old walled bazaar town, the other the Aldershot-style, immaculately laid-out cantonment, with razor-creased khaki drill shorts, bulled boots and Pathan features at almost every barrack gate. The Pearl Continental Hotel sits between the two worlds – 'be careful of the water' – and has the only hotel bar in Pakistan. Filling in the alcohol forms which allow you alcohol in this strict Muslim nation almost deters us from going in, but Nicholas Barrington, the British Ambassador, has given us a bottle of whisky to ease social contacts on our travels. It certainly eases ours.

Peter Rees, head of Afghan Aid, organises a dinner for us at the American Club with a dozen or so other British aid workers to give us an inside picture of Afghanistan. I can see that the Club is a lifeline over the long haul in Peshawar, but there must be evenings when anything is better than this. The bar is humming, or rather shouting, with that distinctively American beer-driven culture that is so disagreeable. The aid workers are young and idealistic, but professional and tough-minded – no illusions about the Mujaheddin, or Pakistani policy, still less US policy. It is best summed up by one worker who says: 'I think that maybe all aid – economic and military – should be cut off so that some sense might be knocked into all the factions.'

More worrying still is the consensus about the deplorable situation within Afghanistan. In summary: irrigation channels have been destroyed; grain has been so degraded that it will have to be renewed to recover; livestock is down to 15 per cent of its original level (at normal rates of recovery it will take 17 years to recover); there are mines everywhere; locusts and two kinds of beetle are devastating the north. The aid workers are, in short, swimming against the tide, and none of them bothers to conceal the fact. It won't stop them doing everything they can to stave off famine and disaster.

12 AUGUST

One of the best sources in Peshawar is Naim Majrooh, who runs the Afghan Information Centre. He took over when his father – the founder – was brutally murdered at his house by a Mujaheddin faction who disliked what he was reporting. Everyone in Peshawar knows who was responsible for the murder. Naim continues the work apparently unperturbed. His analysis is that Jalalabad was a total disaster. It was forced on the Mujaheddin by the Pakistani ISI, the intelligence agency. There was no unified force, no strategic plan, and therefore no tactics to back up the plan. Some 6500 were killed or wounded out of a besieging force of perhaps 30 000. Now there is still no unified command, let alone any strategy. Take the Kabul road. Why did they not cut it? Because they rotated the road-cutting duty among the various groups the road was never cut consistently or at the right time. The airport was closed but no one then pressed on with the road. In addition the rocketing drove out thousands of refugees. Now the government is dug in, defended and supplied, and the Mujaheddin cannot resist their air power. Mujaheddin tactics over Kandahar are a revealing pointer to their attitude. NIFA – the monarchist faction of the Mujaheddin – are said to be planning an attack within a fortnight. Naim asks why 'Kandahar was always good Mujaheddin territory. They had many supporters there; they hid guerrillas; in no sense was it a government city. Why fire in rockets against what are mainly their own people? The arrangement there is so informal that the Mujaheddin check in their weapons when they arrive at the city gate and get them back as they leave as at a cloakroom. These are the kind of unthinking Mujaheddin tactics that are losing not gaining support.'

There are other elements in the picture. Firstly, Najib is not a fundamentalist. He has dropped Marxism-Leninism. He speaks of nationalism – a plus – while the fundamentalists do not. He will not take away from women the rights they enjoy. Why should any one now willingly revert to the Mullahs? Secondly, there is revenge. After one early post-Soviet battle, the defenders were invited to come over to the Mujaheddin. They did. They were slaughtered; few are ready to run such a risk again. Such acts are blamed on the 'Arabs', otherwise known as the Saudi-backed Wahabi, who are very fundamentalist, very murderous, very fanatical. No one explains why they were let in – 'they're just keen boys eager to fight a holy war' – still less why, now they have done such damage, they are allowed to stay. This is another instance of lack of political control.

13 AUGUST

A brief visit to the closest refugee camp to Peshawar, Kancha Garhi, on the Khyber road. It is old-established, with solid mud-walled houses, long streets and winding alleys, and would not be mistaken for a refugee camp if you did not know. All agree they will only return when there is 'victory'; that victory means defeat of 'all the Communists', and they will follow their leaders. Their unanimity speaks volumes for the political control in the camps at least.

Will they ever negotiate? 'Not while there are Communists in the government.' When will they win? 'We will obey our leaders, but they do not speak with one voice. If they spoke with one voice, then everything would happen' – this last damning conclusion from a tall old man whose every other utterance has been one of total loyalty to the leaders of the Jamiat faction of the Mujaheddin.

Back to the house of the Prime Minister of the Interim Government, Professor Mujadidi. He lives in a nondescript back street in west Peshawar. A group of armed men cluster on the verandah. Another prays on a prayer mat. It is suffocatingly hot and humid, even though it is already 5 o'clock in the evening.

Mujadidi's son greets us in a waiting room filled with the deafening blast of a half man-size, floor-standing fan, delivering constant volleys of hot air. The son is an American-trained doctor, wearing coolly elegant, pale blue long shirt and trousers and a crochet cap. His father is similarly clad, but with a turban, and a small gold watch chain across his cotton vest. He is calm, almost too gentle. He delivers an outburst at Gulbuddin Hekmatyar; he must leave the Interim Government; it cannot work with him. 'His behaviour is intolerable; he is a gangster.' He alleges that he has killed more people in Afghanistan than anybody else. His outspokenness is extraordinary. He says the Mujaheddin must have a united cabinet, a unified command within Afghanistan and a successful military campaign before the end of the fighting season. In the end he is very vague, with too little analysis and too much hopefulness presented as policy.

It is a different experience when we visit Professor Rabani, leader of the Jamiat Party, 36 of whose commanders are widely said to have been murdered inside Afghanistan by Gulbuddin Hekmatyar's men. The 'Minister for Information' greets us. He complains about BBC coverage, I say that if their reports were more consistent, more trustworthy, and more verifiable, I have no doubt they would be treated as they deserve. The Minister agrees that their publicity has been confused, contradictory and incredible; he is determined to do better.

Rabani is quiet and academic but far shrewder and more analytical than Mujadidi. Yes, the Russians had handled various things rather cleverly. Firstly they timed their withdrawal for February (i.e. mid-winter), the worst time for the Mujaheddin. Secondly, they supplied the Najibullah government with some $2 billion worth of equipment. Thirdly, the Russians have not 'really' withdrawn; there are still Russian advisers, and they man the Scud missiles. Fourthly, Kabul propaganda was effective and won over international opinion after the Soviet withdrawal. Finally, as a result, international donors thought the war was over and lost interest in Afghanistan. But the war with the Russians goes on.

Then he assesses the Mujaheddin faults. They were so proud to have defeated a superpower that they assumed the leftovers would present no difficulty. (The interpretation is, 'We believed our own propaganda.') He uses the word 'proud' twice. In addition, the Mujaheddin did not think up any tactics before Jalalabad, and military supplies from abroad were cut off about three months before the Soviet withdrawal as if the affair was over. (This may well have been due to the US election handover.) Lastly, their publicity and propaganda was bad and confused.

It is refreshing to hear some hard analysis. But will it make a difference? In all, during a week in Pakistan devoted to talk on this engrossing subject, no one seems to differ from the above consensus. The newspapers have included at least three big features critical of Afghan policy and dubious about its success. There is a rare unanimity but still the policy staggers on. Why?

14 AUGUST

Climax of Afghan mania – a trip across the Khyber Pass. We reach the famous Karkhano Bazaar, a large area of arcaded shops stretching for some several hundred yards on the right of the road leaving Peshawar. The exposed concrete pillars and reinforcing rods sticking up above the roofs indicate their builders' belief that the market will grow. The bazaar specialises in consumer goods, mainly Russian, but is said to be a black market on the grand scale. One shop is called 'Marks and Spencer St Michael', its neighbour 'Mothercare'.

A mile further on both sides of the road are lined with rattan stalls. Each one carries revolvers, ammunition, and raw opium. We buy ten .28 revolver cartridges and fire them off into the air behind the stall. Zulfi, our driver, then produces his more powerful .32 revolver, revealing a shoulder belt of some 30 cartridges, and we fire them off too. The stall-holder offers a large lump of raw opium as big as a fist for 500 rupees. It smells very earthy and slightly damp. It is black and sticky, with a skin like an elephant. Another person approaches Phil Jones and offers him heroin at a price which would make a fortune in London. It is very casual, totally uncontrolled, and ought to seem more evil. But the Western consequences of the drug trade are of no importance whatever to people driven out of their country for a decade. What you witness is a wholly uncontrolled society – arms, drugs, politics are all out of government control.

Before we enter the foot of the Pass we came to the first of the Afridi villages (actually small walled towns, with high smooth mud walls, a watch tower at the corner with tiny rifle slits, one large gate, no decoration, and small decorated points on the top of the wall as a symbolic reminder that they are defences). They blend with the landscape and are harmonious, graceful and strong. Higher up the Khyber they get bigger, more densely crowded. I had no idea the Khyber had so many people in it. These are also the homes of the drug barons. One is brick-built, with two gates, lined with tiles and a barbed-wire fence all round. It is ugly and conspicuous. It is the home of Ayub, named by the government as a drug smuggler. He denies it and says, according to Zulfi, that if the government comes for him and his 300 men 'he has lots of bullets for them'. No one is going to mount a punitive expedition up the Khyber to get him. But he is a house prisoner, as he will be arrested if he sets foot in Peshawar.

We stop opposite one of the only three petrol stations in the Pass. Its owners live opposite in a village whose walls run several hundred yards along the road, 20 feet high, and at least 50 yards deep. The front courtyard is more than 30 square yards, and contains a small mosque, trees, immaculately kept gravel, and an open arcade filled with about a dozen charpoys for visitors. We are ushered into the visiting room for guests. One of the sons of the family appears and talks while tea is brought. He is training to be an engineer; another a doctor; two other cousins enter, they too are destined for university. All speak good English. Their village is made up of one family – there are 135 of them. They grow vegetables for their own use, and much of the village is used for farming as there is plenty of space. Their family is involved in 'business' – transport and suchlike – very vague. Some of it is tyres. They sold their Kabul business as it was too hard to keep it going.

We discuss Ayub, the alleged drugs dealer. 'The government will not attack him because the people are with him,' say the cousins. This is after all Afridi tribal territory where the government's writ runs only 8 feet either side of the road. The cousins have dual Pakistani-Afghani nationality which means they can vote in both countries and are in effect citizens of both. What do they do in the summer? Play indoor games. In winter they ride. Do they climb mountains? No point, there is nothing to hunt. They urge us to have lunch. One reason for traditional Afridi hospitality is undoubtedly boredom. Sadly we have meetings arranged and press on.

Large 'villages', immaculately built and mud-finished, are the main feature of the extraordinary landscape. So is the railway, rising, backing, tunnelling, and all to end up at Turkham right on the Afghan border. The station at Landi Kotal is bleak and open – the train runs just once a week – but that at Turkham, with the rails running into the sand a few yards short of the Afghan border, is one of the world's missed opportunities. Empty railway stations always have their own plangency; a disused one at the end of the line is in its own class.

The road is metallic and Zulfi hammers past the highly decorated lorries and overcrowded Nissan pick-ups. The great landmarks of British rule and fighting stand to this day, well-fitted for the demands of the Khyber: huge fortresses astride hill tops, smaller towers on commanding heights. Frequent signs remind us that this is military country. 'Welcome to the Khyber Rifles' proclaims a large concrete block painted in red; on its top stands a charpoy, cutting the claim down to a domestic scale; elsewhere we see crests where regiments served and died in these craggy defiles. It becomes very narrow on only a few occasions; the problem is that there is nowhere to fight and nowhere to run.

From the last crest we look down a 1000-foot drop to Turkham and the border. To the left, an incredible chain of hill forts and walls at some 6000 feet are linked along the ridge line as if waiting for an assault. In Turkham, a ghost town, there is a large shopping area, bus station and open market – all deserted except for two desperate shopkeepers. The frontier crossing is highly bulled but relaxed. The Pakistani Frontier Rifle guards clatter loudly to the present when a local commander – in civvies – brings his family and children down to see the Mujaheddin.

We stand by the frontier chain and in due course the Mujaheddin appear, as you would expect, armed, bandoliered and bearded. Yes, there has been fighting down the road. Yes, they will win. It is all very predictable. All the groups share control of Turkham on the Afghan side because it was the first town they liberated. But it is all rather unreal and a pale shadow of itself. No one crosses while we are there. The guards give us Coca-Cola, we chat desultorily and make for the return. The mountains are grand, very harsh. How anyone knew there was a way through defeats the imagination. There are easier passes it is said; Akhbar demanded the straightest one. The whole experience is so overwhelming that after seeing it we feel like doing nothing but taking tea with the Governor, Brigadier Gulistan Janjua.

The Governor's House is an elegant classical wood pavilion set in splendid gardens. The drive-in portico has immaculately turned-out Khyber Rifle guards, dressed in exquisite dark grey with red flashes jutting upwards from their turbans (they look like black Redstarts). About three flunkeys take us in – me in my suit, white shirt, tie and Panama hat. About three more flunkeys bow us over from the waiting room to the Governor's study. He is a distinguished man with a small moustache, and perfect Punjabi military English, dressed in traditional Pakistani clothes made from the sheerest cotton or silk in pale khaki, and completed with a silk kerchief of palest turquoise. It is teatime chat: of drugs (he has eradicated most of the poppy fields in North-West Frontier Province); of law and order (yes there is a Kalashnikov culture); of dissolving the assembly (no there is a working majority and he has no need to intervene). He is strongly critical of India, its ambitions stretching from Indonesia to the Oxus, and its restless urge to dominate its neighbours. He points to India's policy towards Bangladesh which is militarily powerless, its trade blockade of Nepal, the military intervention in the Maldives, and the refusal to withdraw after intervening in Sri Lanka. Naturally – in this context – Pakistan is the great obstacle to Indian domination and is resented and resisted as a result. This is all very revealing as an indicator of Pakistani military thinking. He shows us the dining room hung with the names and crests of former Governors of North-West Frontier Province, and the Durbar Room. After inviting us to lunch he takes us right down to the car and personally sees us off. The guards stamp, and we are away down the main cantonment road.

16 AUGUST

Two days later, we are in Chitral, high in the foothills of the Himalayas. We have been taken to the remote and fabulously beautiful Sousoon Valley, where Chitrali villagers live off steep, irrigated hillsides, the water driven by the immense power of the snow-fed rivers. Our guide, Massoud, says we will go into the hotel in Chitral town; his cousin and father are looking after two Americans on a fact-finding visit. One is the Vice-Consul from Peshawar, the other a Congressional staffer from the Budget Committee looking at aid projects. The staffer asks us what people are saying about the Mujaheddin and US policy. We unload two weeks of talking and observations on to him. The overwhelming drift of our comments and observations is deeply critical of American policy. He looks startled; the Vice-Consul looks cross. The staffer asks questions, and we answer. He takes it all in good part, but such extensive criticism of American policy seems to come as a total surprise. As we walk out to our cars he says to my wife: 'Well, there's no danger of your ever being mistaken for an American.'

There are no hard feelings. At dinner in the evening at the Assistant Commissioner's, we sit under huge walnut trees in the warm wind blowing up Chitral Valley and realise why Kipling so fell in love with the place, as he did in his short story 'The Man who Would be King', set in the Calash Valley ten miles away.

17 AUGUST
An early start to get the first plane out of Chitral before any cloud closes the passes. Ann is carrying the remnants of the Ambassadorial bottle of whisky in her hand luggage. Two orthodox Muslim girls in the women's security booth rise from their prayers and reading of the Koran to examine her bags. Clearly a Western woman's handbag is full of special curiosities and its contents are closely and slowly examined. But the whisky causes sheer puzzlement. Is it explosive or dangerous? Ann mimes drinking. The security girl assumes she wants a drink so, at 7.20 am, pours out the stopper full of whisky and mimes to her to drink it. Anxious to please, Ann does so. It does not really help. A male policeman enters. He understands it is whisky and says it should go in the hold baggage which has already been minutely searched, checked and passed through to the plane. I say it is not worth it; it should stay in the hand baggage. 'In that case', says the policeman, 'it must be poured away' and goes straight to the water drinking fountain and pours the bottle down the waste pipe. A German tourist watches in disbelief and horror: 'Du Lieber Gott' he groans.

INDEX